*f*P

Too Many Bosses, Too Few Leaders

The Three Essential Principles You Need

to Become an Extraordinary Leader

Rajeev Peshawaria

FREE PRESS

NEW YORK   LONDON   TORONTO   SYDNEY

FREE PRESS
A Division of Simon & Schuster, Inc.
1230 Avenue of the Americas
New York, NY 10020

First Free Press hardcover edition May 2011

FREE PRESS and colophon are trademarks of Simon & Schuster, Inc.

For information about special discounts for bulk purchases,
please contact Simon & Schuster Special Sales at 1-866-506-1949
or business@simonandschuster.com.

The Simon & Schuster Speakers Bureau can bring authors to your live event.
For more information or to book an event contact the Simon & Schuster Speakers Bureau
at 1-866-248-3049 or visit our website at www.simonspeakers.com.

Designed by Mspace/Maura Fadden Rosenthal

Medical illustrations on page 85 courtesy of iStockphoto.com

Manufactured in the United States of America

10   9   8   7   6   5   4   3   2

Library of Congress Cataloging-in-Publication Data
Peshawaria, Rajeev.
Too many bosses, too few leaders: the three essential principles you need to become an
extraordinary leader / Rajeev Peshawaria.
p. cm.
1. Leadership. I. title.
HD57.7.P47 2011
658.4'092—dc22   2010042147

ISBN 978-1-4391-9774-5
ISBN 978-1-4391-9776-9 (ebook)

To my parents.

Your memory inspires me to this day.

CONTENTS

INTRODUCTION

Mohandas Gandhi started his working life like any other professional and soon became a very successful attorney in the UK. He might have spent the rest of his life practicing law if he had not taken a trip to South Africa on behalf of a client at the age of twenty-four. It was a clear day in South Africa, 1893. Dressed in an elegant suit, Gandhi was traveling first class on a train when he was asked to move to third class because he was "colored." When he produced his ticket to show his right to travel in a first-class compartment, he was asked how he even managed to buy a ticket because only whites were allowed to travel in first class. "I asked for it in the mail," he said, "and as I am a citizen of the British Empire, I should be allowed to travel in first class just like any other citizen regardless of the color of my skin." His protests yielded no results and he was physically thrown out of the train.

Upon meeting with members of the local community, he learned about the extent of segregation of people and life in South Africa. The plight of the people of color, along with his own experience on the train, really moved him. As an attorney, his first response was to legally challenge the validity of certain rules that severely restricted the freedom of colored people. Soon realizing that the goal of obtaining equal status for all people was unlikely to be achieved through litigation, he thought long and hard about what to do. He finally decided that his sole purpose from that point onward would be to champion the cause of equal rights for all. Considering how best to achieve his desired results, he decided that the very unfairness and violence he abhorred would *not* be used as a means to achieve his objectives. Nonviolence would be his vehicle for his fight for freedom and equality. No one could have predicted that a frail brown man in a loincloth would bring down a mighty empire without firing a bullet, yet that is exactly what he achieved.

There are other noteworthy aspects of Gandhi's story. One: Gandhi had no position, title, or formal authority over anyone. He never held any political or military office, did not possess any material wealth, and could not boast of any scientific achievement or extraordinary abilities. Yet millions followed him, were ready to lay down their lives for his cause. Two: Living the way he did was neither comfortable nor glamorous. If he wanted material success and comfort, he would have been much better off as an attorney. He regularly made himself very unpopular, was jailed several times, and was often physically attacked, including the final gunshot that killed him in 1948. Was Gandhi unaware of the dangers involved? Did he do what he did for fame, fortune, and glory? More importantly, how did he manage to achieve the results he wanted without any formal authority or control of resources?

Contrast Gandhi's story with the modern-day manager in the corporate world. In asking bosses all over the world why it is so hard to be a good and effective leader, I have heard a host of reasons, largely due to the increasing complexity of business today. In the good old days, they tell me, the life of a business leader was reasonably straightforward. You had a set of agreed-upon business objectives, a set of direct reports, and the rest of your organization below your direct reports. All the people and resources needed to achieve business objectives were under your control. Aligning people in the pursuit of common goals was straightforward—you controlled both the carrots and the sticks.

They go on to talk about how difficult life in business is today by contrast, and why it is almost impossible to be an effective leader. Below is a sampling of actual quotes from the mouths of surprisingly senior bosses:

- "I live in a highly complicated matrix structure and have long given up trying to make sense of it."

- "I am responsible for achieving results, but have little or no authority over people and resources that are critical for success."

- "I am accountable to three managers."

- "I am responsible for leading the business (P&L, compliance, operations, technology) as well as for leading people (pay, performance, morale). One person cannot possibly do all of it effectively."

- "I have limited control over either carrot or stick."

- "My bonus depends on my 360-degree feedback scores, so I cannot afford to rub too many people the wrong way."

- "The head office, the control department, the strategic planning group, and many other corporate functions make huge demands on my time, leaving me very little time to do my day job."

- " 'Continuous change' is the mantra, and lots of management processes (fads) are introduced regularly to supposedly make our lives easier."

- "My people are constantly looking toward me for answers I simply don't have."

In short, life, according to our current bosses, is a constant struggle to get results without having adequate authority. Isn't it draining just to read their comments?

———————————

"Of all the bosses you've had in your career, how many would you call truly great leaders? For the purpose of this question, a great leader is someone who inspired you to show up every morning and do your best possible work, someone who made you believe in yourself, someone who

genuinely cared about your success, and someone whom you wanted to follow willingly."

As a leadership and management consultant and educator, I have asked this question of thousands of business executives in every continent across a wide range of industries. I have asked groups of senior folks at the twilight of their careers, as well as upcoming middle managers. **Regardless of context, geography, or cultural differences, the average answer in any group lies somewhere between zero and two.** Given the abundance of research and literature on the subject, and the sums invested by companies every year on leadership development, this low average is baffling. Unlike molecular computing or the study of AIDS, leadership is not an evolving science. In fact, the definition of good leadership hasn't changed since the time of Alexander the Great. Why, then, is the average answer so low?

In good economic times (unlike the recession at the time of this writing), one might be tempted to think, "How does it matter? In spite of this low average, companies around the world seem to be doing fairly well." When the going is good, bad leadership often goes undetected. However, consider the next question, which I have asked over the past twenty years, mostly through good times:

"On a one-to-ten scale where ten is at peak potential and one is significantly below potential, how would you rate your organization's current performance in the marketplace?"

Again, I have asked this of a very large number of leaders and teams across the globe. I typically ask this one when I have an entire senior leadership team in a room for a workshop or team meeting. The average answer to this question is roughly 6.5. In other words, barring a few exceptions, the business world, by its own estimate, is operating at 65 percent of its potential. Whichever way you look at it, there is a huge performance void, arguably caused by a leadership void.

According to the American Society of Training and Development (ASTD), U.S. corporations alone spend $134.39 billion every year on employee training. And companies spend an average of 24 percent to 30 percent of their training budgets on leadership development. One has to ask whether this roughly $40.47 billion is being well spent. Most of this training is based on formulas or on emulating successful leaders. Some researchers look at charisma and personality, and prescribe makeover formulas. Others offer copycat strategies in the name of best-practice research. A popular example is the case method, widely used at some of the finest business schools. It has become the "be all, end all" solution for teaching leadership and, in my opinion, is heavily overused. I can understand cases about failure and learning from the situation. If, however, the case is about a success story, and students are asked to emulate the success formula of the protagonist, it is a waste of time because emulation is, by definition, an act of followership, not leadership. Another common practice is creating formulas about human situations, and prescribing behavior steps for each situation. There is no shortage of two-by-two matrices boxing all human situations in one of four types, and telling students to first recognize the situation, then follow the steps. If only the business of human emotions and motivation were that simple. Formulas can program computers but cannot train humans about leading fellow humans. Clearly, the $40 billion investment is missing the mark.

For executives who complain about the increasing complexity of corporate life today, here is a thought: *Leaders achieve extraordinary results in spite of the environment, not because of it.* Effective leaders take it upon themselves to dig deep and find solutions to the most pressing problems of their times. They feel deeply about the inadequacies of current reality and decide to do something about it. They do not wait to be appointed to important positions before doing so. It is their deep desire to change the status quo that makes them leaders. When in trouble, the average modern boss says "If only . . ." and focuses on obstacles. Leaders ask "What if?" and focus on possibilities. They also achieve great results in spite of their own limitations. All leaders are human, and humans are imperfect. Even the greatest of leaders in history had imperfections. This book is not a study of how you can ensure that you and your team or company never run into trouble. There is no way to do that. This book is a study of what great leaders did right even while they had imperfections and faced daunting problems, just like anyone else. For example, how did Howard Schultz create what we know today as the Starbucks Coffee Company out of nothing but a dream? How did he find the resources to grow a commodity company internationally even though he had no breakthrough technology or new science that fulfilled new consumer needs? How did Kiran Bedi, India's first female police officer, create so much positive change in a highly corrupt and male-dominated society? From where did she find the courage to fight single-handedly against armed mobs and powerful politicians? How did Alan Mulally, an outsider to the auto industry, lead such a spectacular turnaround at Ford? Throughout the book, you will find these and a host of other powerful stories about remarkable leadership. My purpose behind telling these stories is not to have you emulate their behavior, but to show you how they each discovered what leadership meant for them, and how they carried out their leadership agenda. Looking at the discovery process of these leaders should give us clues about the questions we need to ask ourselves in order to discover our own leadership.

So how did Gandhi, and how do other great leaders, accomplish so much? With all the investment in leadership development, what is the elusive key to effective leadership? In my view, it is that superior leadership requires incredible amounts of *emotional energy—the power to stay the course despite the most formidable of obstacles*. Emphasis is most often placed heavily on cerebral skills at the expense of appreciating this crucial source of leadership success. Again, leadership is not about competency models, personality traits, or formulas—it is about having the lasting energy to stay true to your vision for positive change even in the face of the most powerful resistance. Leaders who achieve exceptional results despite the toughest of challenges are able to do so because they know how to:

1. Identify sources of unlimited emotional energy to fuel themselves

2. Enlist a few co-leaders and align their energy toward a shared purpose

3. Galvanize the energy of large numbers of people to create sustainable collective success

In other words, leadership is all about energy. I define leadership as **the art of harnessing human energy toward the creation of a better future.** At the end of the day the difference between leaders and nonleaders is this: Leaders find the energy to stay on and fight, and energize others around them, while nonleaders give up. Energy can neither be learned in a classroom nor automatically acquired by accepting a big title or position of authority. Leadership energy must be discovered, and there is no shortcut to the discovery process. This book is all about how to discover your own leadership energy and how to help others in finding theirs.

In over twenty-two years at global blue-chip organizations, including American Express, HSBC, Goldman Sachs, Coca-Cola, and Morgan Stanley, I have learned a great deal about energizing oneself, enlisting and aligning co-leaders, and galvanizing the troops. I have held both line and staff jobs, and have managed large global teams in eight countries. Besides leading global teams myself, I have worked closely with some of the most famous corporate leaders of our times. For example, I watched closely as John Mack led his team through the toughest crisis in Morgan Stanley's storied history, and how he eventually saved the firm, while Dick Fuld, his neighbor across the street, was unable to do the same for Lehman Brothers. I also watched how Neville Isdell turned the Coca-Cola Company around at a time when two prior CEOs had less success. For twelve years, I observed how Harvey Golub and Ken Chenault delivered against the core mission of American Express— *to be the world's most respected service brand*—and brought the company back on a solid footing for sustainable growth. Later, while creating various training experiences for clients, I studied leaders like Jeff Bezos of Amazon.com, Jack Ma of Alibaba.com and Tom Gardner of The Motley Fool. You will read about all of these leaders throughout this book. Their success had nothing to do with their personality or with the management techniques they used. They all had one thing in common: They were deeply moved by the inadequacies of current reality and wanted to do something about it. Furthermore, they were able to find the endless energy needed to stay the long course despite the formidable resistance. After finding their own sources of energy, they were able to energize others around them. Together with their teams, they harnessed human energy toward the creation of a better future.

My experience has taught me that there are several core principles regarding good leadership, which apply across all cultures and in all areas of business. A key question about leadership is, how do some leaders manage to stay in control and focused on their leadership agenda, while others buckle under the slightest of pressure? The first principle is that staying focused comes from maintaining your personal leadership energy, and that the only foolproof way to find, channel, and sustain your energy is to *clearly define your purpose and your values*. A fundamental purpose and associated set of values are the sources of personal energy, and once you develop laser-sharp clarity about them, you will have created a strong foundation for leading and earned the right to advance to the next phase of leadership—energizing others. In the first chapter of this book, I will lay out a simple set of questions that will help you define your purpose and values. No one disagrees when I say that the very foundation of leadership is to have full clarity of purpose and values. However, very few leaders are able to clearly describe their purpose and values when asked. The usual response I get is, "Hmm . . . That is a very deep question. No one has ever asked me that . . ." Coming as it does from very senior leaders, I find this response unacceptable. How can you call yourself a leader if you haven't thought about your purpose and values? And you were waiting to be asked?

The second principle gets to the bottom of what leaders need to do to enlist and energize key influencers around them, one at a time. The world is far too complex for any one leader to have all the answers. We need a team of co-leaders around us if we want to create a better future. This principle deals with what leaders need to do to enlist co-leaders in the journey. At the core of the principle is the insight that nobody can motivate another person because every individual comes premotivated. This does not mean, however, that a leader can't do anything to channel and harness that motivation to optimal effect. The good news is that, regardless of culture or industry, each individual has expectations for their work that fall into three buckets—*Role, Environment, and Development (RED)*. We all have questions about our workplace:

1. **What is my *Role*?** Is it meaningful? Does it align with my personal purpose? Is it challenging enough? Will it allow me to make a useful contribution to something bigger? Will it utilize my strengths?

2. **What is my work *Environment* like?** Is it one that treats people with respect and dignity? Is it fun? Is it a meritocracy? Are my coworkers smart and capable? Do we have a common set of core beliefs? Are they (those beliefs) in line with my personal values?

3. **How will I *Develop* and grow?** Will I have opportunities to learn and develop? Will I be able to try out new things? Will I get coaching and feedback? Will my manager take a personal interest in my career?

While the emphasis that each person places on one versus another of these may differ, each bucket is always a factor in their level of energy and engagement to some degree. In the second chapter of the book, I introduce a method for leading your team that taps into the power of RED. I provide a checklist you can use to help identify people's expectations, and introduce a simple, time-efficient way to get to the bottom of every employee's needs. To lead effectively, you must understand the people you lead.

The third core principle is that as a leader, your job is not to directly produce results, it is to create the conditions that will galvanize the energy of others to facilitate sustainable collective success. Chapters 3 to 6 show how to invigorate an entire enterprise or organization. Once you move beyond the level of leading a co-located team of direct reports to leading an entire department, division, company, or organization, you may be leading hundreds or thousands of people. At this level, you have more than two layers of hierarchy below you—i.e., you have several managers in your organization. I call this the "enterprise leadership level." Now, it is impossible to directly supervise and motivate everyone. You simply cannot be everywhere at the same time. What, then, should you personally focus on in order to give your business the maximum advantage? What actions should you spend your time on and where should you delegate? I provide a powerful framework—*brains-bones-nerves*—that will focus your time on the three most important levers for business success, which as a leader you must shape and control.

In chapter 7, I tell the stories of a few exceptional leaders and how each has followed these fundamental principles in achieving extraordinary success. A common theme runs through all of the stories: The leaders first found their own leadership energy by clarifying their personal purpose and values; then enlisted a few co-leaders on the journey; and finally galvanized the entire organization toward shared purpose and values by focusing on the most important leadership actions.

My research repeatedly confirmed that the main cause of sustained success of any organization is the proactive practice (by the senior leadership team) of the three core principles above. However, I also found that even the best of companies slip up from time to time. And this slipping is attributable to the same top management team that achieved the prolonged success. Further investigation into several companies that experienced such downturns revealed that in each case the failure was the result of leaders taking their eyes off the ball, becoming too comfortable in their role or about the strength of their organization's culture, systems, and structures. In other words, when the leaders stopped applying the three principles in a proactive way, their organizations ran into turbulence. Recent examples are major Wall Street firms that perhaps became complacent about their risk-management processes and systems; Toyota, a company revered over decades for its high quality standards, which found itself grappling with one of its biggest recalls in history; Coca-Cola—whose market leadership withered between the death of Roberto Goizueta and the arrival of Neville Isdell. I will tell some stories of such failure along the way in this book, because they have so much to say about how vital it is to be vigilant in applying the principles I outline.

While most of the stories in this book are based on true incidents, I have often changed names or created composites from multiple incidents.

My goal in this book is not to teach you leadership. Nobody can. But what I can do is give you a proven framework for defining and developing your own leadership agenda, and the tools to enable you to enlist the effective support of others toward realizing that agenda. Participants in my leadership seminars around the world have applied the methods I have developed to their businesses or nonprofit organizations and have experienced significant improvements in organizational performance. Some have commented that applying these tools yielded the highest return ever on time invested. I wrote this book in response to requests from many who desired a one-stop destination or leadership "tool kit" that would help them to further absorb the lessons and teach them to their staff. I hope that you find the methods as valuable as have the thousands of those I've seen benefit so substantially from them.

ACKNOWLEDGMENTS

This book is the result of years of interaction with business leaders around the world. First as a banker and later as a leadership and management consultant, I have learned from more people than is possible to list. It is therefore hard to tell precisely who contributed to the various ideas in the book. Perhaps the biggest contributors were the participants in my training programs and seminars, and senior leadership teams that I coached over the years in their efforts to lead positive change. Most of the ideas and tools were tested on them and refined based on their feedback.

In addition to all those I have learned from and cannot list, several people over the past couple of years have contributed significantly toward making the book a reality. First and foremost, I want to mention Lucinda Blumenfeld, my agent, without whom this work would not be possible. Not only did she believe in the concepts of the book from day one; she worked tirelessly with me to help improve each chapter, often offering tough feedback in the process. Emily Loose, my editor, took it from where Lucinda left off and worked with various drafts until we got it right. Her eye for detail and her constructive criticism went a long way toward making the final product much more readable.

I cannot fail to mention Todd Obolsky and Susan E. B. Schwartz, my research team members, for their valuable contributions, particularly with a couple of stories in chapter 7. They delivered great work at short notice under considerable deadline pressure.

Without the moral support and encouragement of family and friends, I would never have been able to get to the finish line. I want to thank Rajendra Kumar for going through several drafts and giving valuable feedback and encouragement; Vandana, Salim, and Kabir

Peshawaria for putting up with me as I worked on the manuscript; and Kiran Bedi, who as a role model was my inspiration to go on each time I felt tired or disheartened. Last but not least, I want to thank the staff of the ICLIF Leadership & Governance Center for their understanding and support while I was busy finalizing the manuscript.

Too Many Bosses,
Too Few Leaders

PART ONE

Self- and Team Leadership

1

ENERGIZE the Self: Self-Leadership

Imagine you are twenty-four years old. It is the 1980s and you have just been offered a promotion to a highly visible job in a prestigious international bank headquartered in New York. The new job entails the opportunity to travel the world in first class, and to work closely with a very influential senior person who could help boost your career in the years to come. You enjoy both the prestige and the substance of your current job at the bank, but this new opportunity offers you a chance to succeed in ways you never thought possible. Imagine also that you grew up in a middle-class family with humble means, and that you still have student loans to repay. Now think about what you would do if, even as you are considering this new job, someone suggests you instead quit working at the bank to work as an ambassador of African women at the African Development Bank, focusing on women's development?

Even if you had dreams of making a difference and helping the underprivileged, conventional wisdom would suggest focusing on building a successful career first, then using your wealth and your power to make a difference later. However, if you were Jacqueline

Novogratz, founder and CEO of the Acumen Fund, you would go to Africa instead.

When Jacqueline was just six, she dreamed about changing the world. When she told Sister Theophane, her teacher at the Catholic school she attended, that she wanted to become a nun, she learned a lesson that she never forgot. "Regardless of what you become," said Sister Theophane, "always remember, to whom much is given, much is expected. God gave you many gifts and it is important that you use them for others as best you can." From then on, Jacqueline continued to clarify her thinking and ask herself what she wanted out of life. When she reached the point where she had to decide between Africa and Chase Manhattan Bank, her choice was clear. By this time, she was beginning to acquire greater clarity about the two most important foundations of personal leadership—her purpose and her values. This clarity gave her the energy needed to embark upon an unexpected course, and to stay the course despite the difficulties involved. The more I read about Jacqueline, the more impressed I became with her as a leader. I wanted to know where she finds her energy, how she manages to stay the course despite everything that comes her way, and how she motivates the people who work at Acumen. So I arranged to meet with her for a long interview.

From the moment I started talking with Jacqueline, I could feel her energy. I started by asking her to define her purpose, and her face immediately lit up with excitement. Her enthusiasm for her work was so strong that I could not help but feel energized myself. I had to hold back my urge to tell her how impressed I was with her vision and her work, and how much I wanted to help. "The metapurpose," she said, "is to create a world in which everyone, including the poorest of people, have access to affordable, quality goods and services so they can make their own choices. I have a deep, deep belief that dignity comes from choice, and the vision is a world where people have the ability to make their own choices. We are trying to achieve this vision through Acumen, which combines small amounts of philanthropic capital with large doses of business acumen and innovation to build enterprises that serve vast numbers of the poor—providing them critical goods and services like health care, water, housing, and energy, at affordable prices. So while Acumen is the tactical vehicle to achieve the purpose, the actual purpose is much more spiritual."

Today, Acumen invests philanthropic capital in social enterprises around the world, mostly in the form of loans or equity, to help build organizations that can sustain themselves financially over the long term while providing solutions to the problems of extreme poverty. Based on the belief that pure charitable aid misses the mark and often creates corruption, Acumen operates in the space between pure charity and pure commerce. Using the rigor and expertise of for-profit businesses, Acumen invests in and helps social enterprises become successful and self-sufficient. By lending money instead of granting it, and by providing other support in terms of business planning, hiring, and marketing, Acumen builds metrics for success into the plan, and holds entrepreneurs accountable for delivering results. From its humble beginnings in 2001 with seed capital from the Rockefeller Foundation, Cisco Systems Foundation, and three individual philanthropists, Acumen has grown into a $50 million fund financing and guiding social enterprises in the United States, United Kingdom, Tanzania, Kenya, Pakistan, India, and East Africa. Jacqueline built Acumen brick by brick through years of unwavering resolve and hard work. I asked her how she found the energy to stay the course despite all the obstacles and dangers she faced along the way, and she said, "Among other things, it was by constantly reminding myself about what I am on this earth to do."

I wanted to know how Jacqueline conceptualized and ultimately settled on her purpose. It became clear as she narrated some early experiences. When Jacqueline started her career at Chase Manhattan Bank, she attended the bank's rigorous credit training program. Soon after the program, she joined a group of sixty young bankers in a department called Credit Audit, and traveled the world to examine the quality of the bank's loans, especially in troubled economies. It was during these travels (to Latin America and elsewhere) that she first experienced the coexistence of extreme poverty and vast wealth, and began to feel a strong desire to make a difference. Wherever she looked, the gap between the rich and the poor was stunning, and she began to think about ways in which the poor could also have opportunities to succeed. She started at the obvious place, her own bank, and asked her boss about investing at least some capital in lending to the poor. Predictably, that conversation went nowhere. Her boss argued that the high transaction costs of small loans and lack of collateral among the poor made such a business unfeasible. In addition, the poor were entrapped by a "culture of poverty" and that meant that no one would repay the loans. The conversation only increased Jacqueline's resolve. As I have said before, the difference between leaders and bosses is that while leaders are deeply moved by the inadequacies of current reality and decide to do something about them against all odds, bosses (or nonleaders) learn to cope with the present and don't do anything about it. Clearly, Jacqueline was a leader in the making and wasn't going to stop at one rejection. Soon after this meeting with her boss, she resigned from her job and decided to join the African Development Bank and head out to Africa. She had all kinds of doubts about giving up a lucrative career, and about losing the prestige of being an international banker, but the dream of making a real difference trumped those fears. During her two years in Africa, she faced no shortage of challenges, including a bout of malaria, threats to her safety, language barriers, and the lack of connectivity to the outside world in those pre-Internet days. Yet, by the time she boarded the plane back home, she had started the first bank for the poor in Rwanda, quadrupled the daily income of a group of women running a small bakery business, and learned a great deal. Her experiences in Africa further strengthened her resolve to combine business and charity as a more powerful way to address the problems of poverty.

To prepare herself for the next phase of life, she joined the Stanford MBA program. After finishing business school, she joined the Rockefeller Foundation, where she stayed for nine years before starting Acumen. When she discussed with Sir Gordon Conway, then president of the Rockefeller Foundation, her idea of creating a different kind of institution, one that straddled the best lessons of philanthropy and proven business approaches, she received a very different response from that given by her boss at Chase Manhattan years earlier. She explains the meeting as follows in her book, *The Blue Sweater: Bridging the Gap Between the Rich and the Poor in an Interconnected World:*

> "How different is it from the work of foundations today?" he asked.
>
> The biggest difference, I said, is that we wouldn't simply make grants, but we would invest in entrepreneurs who have vision and ability to solve local problems with market-driven ideas and approaches. We would hire creative people with the ability to read financial statements and balance sheets, not just budgets. We wouldn't focus on specific projects, but instead direct our efforts toward building strong organizations that we would gradually help bring to financial sustainability.

To her surprise, Gordon asked her to take a few months to explore the idea while still working at the foundation. At the same time, another alternative arose. A major financial institution approached Jacqueline to build a $100 million-plus philanthropic program for its clients. Again she was faced with a difficult choice. The philanthropic program offered her access to people of power, plentiful financial resources, and seven times her salary at the Rockefeller Foundation. On the other hand, there was the freedom of building the Acumen Fund—exactly what she wanted to do, although it involved a lot of uncertainty and risk. Needless to say, she chose the latter, and began raising money to start Acumen. Despite the abundance of naysayers, by early 2001, Jacqueline and her founding team had created a business plan and had raised $8 million in philanthropic capital. Soon they began investing in the ideas of social entrepreneurs in India, Pakistan, and Africa. Today, the fund manages over $50 million in capital, and is making a serious difference in the lives of the people in communities where they invest. To fully understand the work and the impact of Acumen, consider just two examples.

India's 650,000 rural villages house approximately 71 percent of the country's 1.1 billion people. Most of them live without easy access to trade, government, business, and health services. To access information available at the fingertips of the urban population, villagers need to travel long distances, often forgoing daily wages in the bargain. There are no telephones or computer and Internet services available in most villages. This makes it easy for intermediaries to demand hefty cuts and high fees to enable villagers to participate in the country's economy.

The increased availability of information and communication technologies can significantly help rural populations to participate more actively in the economy, and to receive fairer remuneration for their goods and services without having to go through corrupt intermediaries who extort from them. Drishtee.com, a social enterprise dedicated to helping the rural poor, is in the process of establishing a network of tele-kiosks, one in each village, to alleviate this problem. A tele-kiosk is a small office operated by a local entrepreneur, and usually has a phone, a computer, and a camera. Villagers walk up to the kiosk to get a range of services like accessing information on current crop prices, receiving computer training classes, or making long-distance calls. The kiosk operator charges a small fee for the services, and shares a part of the profit with Drishtee. In return for connecting them to consumers, Drishtee also receives a commission from service providers like telecom operators and crop buyers. According to Satyan Mishra, CEO of Drishtee—which means "vision" in Hindi—every dollar spent on connecting the country's 300 million poorest citizens to the national economy yields twenty dollars of social benefit. With several thousand kiosks already established, Drishtee's vision is to provide kiosks for each one of India's 650,000 villages. Acumen has invested a total of $1.6 million ($1 million in the form of equity and $600,000 as debt) in Drishtee to help facilitate the expansion of the tele-kiosks. In early 2008, Drishtee began expanding more quickly than Starbucks did in its early years, opening about four kiosks a day. By the fall of that year, the company was operating in more than four thousand villages, creating more than 5,300 jobs and serving 7.5 million people.

Another of Acumen's impressive contributions is preventing deaths caused by malaria. The disease kills anywhere from one to two million people each year, 90 percent of whom are in Africa. While there were many reasons for the spread of malaria in Africa, the nonavailability of affordable bed nets was certainly one of them. If insecticide-treated bed nets were more easily available to people, they would help keep malaria-carrying mosquitoes away and allow people to sleep more peacefully.

Sumitomo Chemical Company of Japan had already developed a method of impregnating a polyethylene-based netting material with organic insecticide and created a bed net that could last five years. The challenge was to find a manufacturer in Africa that could take this new technology and produce these bed nets locally. Acumen's team not only identified A to Z Textiles as the company to do this, but also provided a loan for the first bed-net weaving machines. With Acumen's initial help, Anuj Shah, CEO of A to Z, went on to ultimately employ more than seven thousand women to produce 16 million nets a year, saving thousands of lives.

These are just two of a host of examples of the positive changes that Jacqueline's Acumen Fund is helping create. Jacqueline is a perfect case in point of how once you are clear about your personal sources of energy, virtually no obstacle will be insurmountable. Very early on in her life, she began to ask herself what she really wanted to achieve and what principles would guide her pursuits. Once she attained clarity on those issues, there was no looking back. "I did not want to become old at 35, and knew instinctively that a combination of service and adventure could lead to a life of passion and constant renewal," she writes in *The Blue Sweater.*

The old saying is true: Lead yourself to lead others. One of the biggest reasons for the abundance of poor or mediocre leaders is that people accept leadership positions for the wrong reasons. They either do so for personal fame, fortune, or glory or are picked to fill positions of leadership based on technical expertise alone. They fail to ask some critical questions about themselves. Gandhi chose the path of leadership not because he wanted personal fame or fortune, but because he believed in his purpose and wanted to harness the power of millions toward achieving it. He fully understood the dangers involved and knew he would create a lot of conflict by painting a picture of a better future. Yet he willingly created the conflict and had the courage to act according to his values in the face of grave danger.

Leadership is not about personal fame or fortune alone. There is nothing wrong with working for self-interest, most of us do, but leadership needs a purpose bigger than self-interest. Personal fame and fortune should be a by-product of leadership, not an end in itself. It is not a popularity sport. People who go into a leadership position without fully understanding this end up being dissatisfied with their lives, and make terrible bosses. I am not proposing selfless pursuit here. All I am suggesting is this: If personal gain is the primary goal, there are other avenues to achieve it—those that don't involve leading and managing others. Leadership and management often require putting self-interest on the back burner in order to achieve results for the greater good.

Unfortunately, the only way to advance your career in most companies is to take on more managerial/leadership responsibility. If you fail to ask yourself if leadership is for you, and if you fail to carefully consider what is involved in being a leader of others, it can easily become a very difficult experience for both you and your subordinates. Do you know of someone who became a parent by accident when they really did not want to be one? Can you imagine how miserable life can be for both the child and the parent in this case? There is no guaranteed reward (fame, fortune, or glory) at the end of the parenting journey. The reward is in the journey itself. Most people realize this and cherish every moment of their parenting journey—the good as well as the difficult. Leadership is like parenting. The reward needs to be in the journey. Accepting a leadership position without carefully considering what you really want for yourself and for the people around you is a very dangerous proposition.

PERSONAL ENERGY

So how does one energize oneself? The first step is to clearly identify one's personal sources of energy, and as I've said, the underlying sources for all of us are our purpose and values.

Gaining clarity about them isn't as simple as one might think; it calls for a very high level of self-awareness. Far too many people go through life without really knowing what they want out of it. They seem clueless about what is important to them, and end up living a very reactive existence. Have you ever worked for an unpredictable and volatile boss? Chances are you were working for someone who was very unaware of his or her own purpose and values. When you are unaware of your own larger purpose and values, every situation feels like a matter of life and death, and you have little control over your emotions—hence the volatile behavior. Laser-sharp clarity on purpose and values forms the basis of a high level of self-awareness, which, in turn, is the very foundation of leadership.

Having a purpose, and the values to guide you in pursuing it, is so important to true leadership because in its essence, leadership is about creating a future that is better than the present. Doing so first requires that you imagine that better future. Without clarity of personal purpose, it is virtually impossible to imagine a better future. Once a clear picture of the desired future takes shape in your mind, the next step is to determine the values that will guide you while pursuing it. Together, your purpose and values define your leadership identity, and give you the energy you need to stay the course. Just as an architect designs a building before actually building it, you need to proactively design your leadership identity.

Think for a moment about when you worked long and hard and achieved something exceptional in the end. It could be something work related like redesigning a whole process or function, a community project, or even a recreational project like climbing a mountain or giving a performance of some sort. Chances are you had a clear picture in your mind about the future you were trying to create. Chances are you were also clear about the values and principles you would use to resolve difficult dilemmas. Surely, you must have faced a lot of resistance and difficulty while pursuing your goal. Did you feel tired at times? Did you feel like giving up at times? At such times through the journey, how did you reenergize yourself? My guess is, each time you felt overwhelmed by the difficulties involved, you reminded yourself of the future you were trying to create and visualized the end result. It was the visualization of anticipated success that kept you going. If you had to make a difficult decision, you probably dug into your values for guidance. This is how clarity of purpose and values gives you energy. Purpose and values are lasting, almost limitless sources of energy. For sure, the lure of huge monetary rewards or the need to secure yourself against a threat of some kind will energize you to act, but such sources are finite and temporary. Leadership is about the long haul, and you need lasting sources of energy.

Unfortunately, no one can teach you your purpose and values. The reason why the multibillions spent each year on leadership development and training are a complete waste is that most leadership programs look at personality and character traits of great leaders from the past and try to get participants to emulate them. They often create simplistic models of behavior and have participants engage in role-play–based practice sessions. But as I've said, copying someone else's behavior or personality is not leadership. There is no shortcut formula to becoming a better leader.

The only way to define your purpose and values is to ask yourself some tough questions and answer them honestly. Answers may not come to you right away, so you have to keep asking the questions until you find the answers that are right for you. I wish I had a simple formula which would help you do this quickly, but I don't. It will take you a considerable amount of time to get clear on these questions, but I can guarantee that this will be the best investment of time you will ever make. Among other things, it will bring you inner peace because it will help you put things in perspective. People who don't have such clarity are rarely peaceful, and if you are not at peace, you cannot be an effective leader.

Here are the questions that I've found are most effective in gaining clarity. The first three questions will help to define your purpose, and the last three help to define values. I'll list them all first and then go into more detail about each.

1. What few things are most important to me?

2. Do I want to:

   a. lead a simple life rich with everyday small pleasures

   b. achieve great success in an individual endeavor, *or*

   c. lead others toward a better future, *or*

   d. do something entirely different with my life?

3. What results do I want to bring about?

4. How do I want people to experience me?

5. What values will guide my behavior?

6. What situations cause me to feel strong emotions?

PURPOSE

1. What few things are most important to me?

Here, we need to make a brutally honest assessment of what it is we really want. Is it money, hard work, leisure, fun, learning, being liked, being a good spouse or parent, being a good manager, making a difference to others, service, integrity, or something else? Having clarity on the three to five most important things greatly helps in putting your finger on your life purpose.

Clarity on what is important to you has a direct bearing on one of the most common challenges of living the corporate existence—work–life balance—something a lot of executives complain about these days. I find the debate about work versus life very interesting. It is almost as if work is not life, and that you can only have one of the two, or more of one at the expense of the other. The only way to achieve balance is to be clear on what is important to you. People who don't have this clarity can never achieve work–life balance, even if they work in a company with flexible work arrangements. The very term "work–life balance" seems to suggest that when one is working, one is not living. This is indeed a very unhappy situation, but contrary to conventional wisdom, it has nothing to do with the number of work hours in a day or with working conditions. I have known many people who worked extremely long hours, yet had very meaningful personal lives. I also know many others who spent far fewer hours "working," yet lived very satisfying professional lives. The trick in either case is to know what you really want.

I once coached someone who was on the cusp of a major promotion at an investment banking firm. All that seemed to matter to him was making it to managing director—that coveted title on Wall Street telling people you've arrived. I began by asking him to describe the work he liked most and the work he liked least in his job. Each time he told me of the times he had been on television to share his views on markets, his eyes would light up. Each time he would talk about working with anything that involved communication or public affairs, I noticed a passion in his voice. But when he talked about what he did for most of his day, he came across flat at best. Something told me he wasn't clear about his overall purpose and/or values—what he really wanted to do with his life—or at least that he had not thought about them proactively. While he seemed fixated on his possible promotion to MD, it didn't seem as though he had considered what he really wanted to do with his career or personal life. In the absence of clarity on what he really wanted out of life, the short-term goal of making MD had become a be-all-end-all situation for him. It worried me that should he not make it for some reason, he would be totally devastated without realizing that there were probably better opportunities for him doing something else.

I gave him the six questions and asked that he set up our next meeting after he had reflected upon them. He took one quick look at the questions and said, "I don't want to think about these questions." Surprised, I asked him why, to which he responded, "I am scared. I have worked at this firm for twelve years; this is the only place I've worked since college. I don't know the outside world. What will I do if these questions point me toward something outside this firm and this industry? I will not know what to do. I am scared." I empathized with him, told him I understood his concern, and asked, "What if it were true—that your real passion and purpose is somewhere other than your current world—would you rather find out now or after another five years?" I left it to him to decide if he wanted to answer my six questions or not, and told him to call me either way in a couple of weeks.

He called me two weeks later and set up a meeting. When we met, he said he had thought long and hard, and concluded that he did not enjoy his work and wanted to move full-time into financial journalism. He began to thank me for helping him realize his true passion and told me that the next promotion to MD was not that important to him anymore. I was happy for him that he was beginning to define his purpose, but also wanted to make sure that his new purpose was what he really wanted. I advised him not to abandon his quest for MD, to continue to work hard toward it, and keep thinking about his new passion. I said, "If after making MD in six months, you still feel passionate about changing careers to financial journalism, you should definitely do so." I wanted to make sure he got the coveted award under his belt so that he did not have regrets. He did exactly as advised, made MD in six months, and left his firm a few months later. He now works in the financial media industry and often tells me how much "richer" he is even though he makes less money than before.

Had he not asked himself the questions, I am not sure he would have made the change.

Once you've identified the most important things in your life, the next step is to take a very serious look at how being a leader will either allow you to focus on those important things or perhaps pull you away from them. Deliberating over the second question will help toward this.

2. Do I want to:

    a. lead a simple life rich with everyday small pleasures

    b. achieve great success in an individual endeavor, *or*

    c. lead others toward a better future, *or*

    d. do something entirely different with my life?

The first thing to get clear on here is if you want to be a leader at all or not. There is nothing wrong with leading a simple life rich with every-day small pleasures. You need to be honest with yourself—something that sounds obvious, but very often people are not. My friend Johannes in Germany was very clear that he wanted neither to be a leader of oth-ers nor to achieve great heights of success at a solo endeavor. He loved nature, outdoor sports, and adventure travel. He knew right from a young age that he did not want an overly demanding career so that he could devote as much time to his hobbies as possible. I have known him for over twenty-five years, and he hasn't changed his habits one bit. He is an executive at an engineering firm and is very content with his job; in fact, he loves it because it gives him ample opportunity to devote free time to his passions. One of his favorite sports is scuba div-ing. Even after years of diving all over the world, his eyes light up and you can sense the joy in his voice as he describes his most recent dive. Each time I hear him talk about his travels or his sports, I cannot help feeling envious because he sounds so happy with his life. Judging by any yardstick, I think he has built a very successful life for himself.

He is the perfect example of someone who knows what he wants from life and enjoys the everyday small pleasures to the maximum. I have rarely met anyone as "rich" as he is.

But if you aren't like Johannes and you are interested in leadership, you first need to choose between options B and C—self-leadership or leading others. As the term suggests, self-leadership is about driving yourself hard to produce results individually. Here, you dig deep into your own energy and persevere against all odds. Leading others (option C) is about channeling the energy of others and acting as a conductor. Similar to parents who toil for a lifetime to raise good children, sometimes leaders who drive results through others do not even get recognized for their hard work. But they are OK with this because they are ambitious less about themselves and more about collective results. The point is, one needs to be clear about what one prefers.

According to BodyBuildingUniverse.com, Arnold Schwarzenegger was once asked why he picked bodybuilding over any other sport. He said he preferred it over other sports because "I didn't like the fact that I couldn't be personally gratified." He tried other endeavors: track and field, boxing, javelin throw, and weight lifting. But only when his coach suggested he try working with weights to strengthen his legs did Arnold find his true vocation. When he first walked into a gym he was literally awed. As he wrote in his book *Education of a Bodybuilder,* "I found myself in a gym, in awe of muscles I had never seen before and of which I didn't even know the correct name. The bodybuilders were powerful, Herculean. Before my very eyes, my true future opened up: I had found the answer I had been looking for." Thus began, when he was sixteen, the career of the greatest bodybuilder of all time, the man who would be crowned Mr. Olympia for a record seven times. There is no doubt in my mind that he was able to endure years of hard training and sacrifice because (first and foremost) he found total clarity about what he wanted. To him, it was all about achieving greatness in an individual endeavor.

You need to know very clearly what you want out of life. As stated earlier, leading others is neither easy nor glamorous. The key question here is, in the interest of greater good, are you willing to put self-interest on the back burner and focus more on others' success? That is the true essence of leading others. Leading others is not better or worse than self-leadership, it is a preference and requires a different orientation—one that focuses more on others and less on the self. Do you want to be a soccer player or a singles tennis player?

If you indeed want to lead others, you must want to be a team player. Most companies try to teach the value of teamwork. Like leadership, teamwork cannot be taught. You either want to be a team player, which means sharing credit with others, or you don't. Neither is right or wrong, it's just a preference.

3. What results do I want to create?

Whether you choose self-leadership or leading others, here you visualize the future in terms of results you want to create. Visualizing a better future is the basic prerequisite of leadership. Leaders look at issues and opportunities today and visualize a future that addresses the issues or exploits the opportunities. According to Robert Quinn, author of *Deep Change,* you become a leader when you move from problem solving to purpose finding. Leaders take it upon themselves to create a better future, and motivate others to join them on the journey. Gandhi made freedom and equality his main purpose, and decided to galvanize millions of people toward the achievement of his purpose by making it a shared purpose. In business, it is easy to find many managers and bosses who are excellent problem solvers and great at follow-through. But few challenge the status quo and visualize a new and different future. Even fewer invite their teams to participate in brainstorming sessions about how to challenge conventional wisdom and create something different.

I learned the beauty and power of visualizing success early on in my career when I worked for a manager who would often get us all together and ask us to imagine that we were the best team in the world at our work. "What would it look like? What can we do that others are

not even thinking about?" he would ask. By making us visualize success, he would push us to come up with steps that would make it happen. "How should we execute? What will the major obstacles be?" He
would keep pushing until we had not only a compelling vision but also
an executable strategy. I remember feeling energized as a junior member of his team each time he involved us in such an exercise. I pushed
myself hard to come up with new ideas to make the team more successful. That often meant I was given more work, but I willingly took
on more. I found the energy within me to do more because the visualization of success was so stimulating. This is a simple insight, but surprisingly few leaders use it. I have used it repeatedly as a leader and it
never fails me. It also takes a lot of the burden off my shoulders—now
I don't have to have all the answers as a leader. Involving my team in
this manner is an all-out win-win.

Good leaders have a natural tendency to question the status quo.
Kiran Bedi, whom we will meet in more detail in chapter 5, was the
first woman to become an elite police officer in India, in the 1970s.
Known for her integrity and courage, she made policing and prison
reform her purpose. She was deeply moved by the inadequacies of
India's criminal justice system. According to her, the system focused
exclusively on punishing criminals, making no effort to reform them.
Furthermore, the system did not do enough to prevent crime in the first
place—it was only reactive. She decided to use her time as an officer
to change the system into one that gave criminals a chance to become
responsible citizens once again.

In a male-dominated world where corruption was rampant and
working conditions inhuman, it was hard, if not impossible, to achieve
what she set out to do, but she never gave up. Each time she found herself in a difficult situation, she dug into her purpose and values and
found remarkable energy to fight the fight. Legend has it that as she
was leading a small police unit to control a large religious mob armed
with swords, her outnumbered colleagues (all men) ran away, fearing
for their lives. Alone, and armed only with a baton, she fought the mob
single-handedly until more help arrived and the mob was finally con-

trolled. When asked on national television how she did it despite her petite size, she said she had the power of determination by her side. She knew it was the right thing to do, and she just did it.

As she continued to clean up corruption and stop much malpractice, she clearly began to upset certain government officials and ministers. As the officer in charge of traffic control in New Delhi, she even towed away then prime minister Indira Gandhi's car when it was parked in a no-parking zone. Many officials tried to "fix" her and demoralize her by transferring her to insignificant postings or by spreading untrue allegations about her, but she carried on despite the toughest of obstacles, eventually winning the Asian equivalent of the Nobel Peace Prize—the Ramon Magsaysay Award—for her work in transforming the Tihar Jail in New Delhi from a violent dead end into a place where criminals made responsible new beginnings.

For a woman in India during those times to have achieved what she did under the circumstances is exceptional. She was able to do it first because she was very clear about her purpose, and second because she had the courage to act according to her values. Her fame and fortune were the by-products of her leadership, not the other way around. While there are many women in the Indian police force today, Kiran finally retired in 2008 as the highest-ranking female officer in history. Through her nonprofit work aimed at educating rural women and rehabilitating drug addicts and former criminals today, she continues to help those in need and inspire millions to step up to a cause without worrying about resources or power.

VALUES

Purpose defines what you want to create, and values define how you will create it. The next three questions will help you to define your core values. Knowing your values, and having conviction about them, is extremely important for great performance, particularly as leaders. Simply put, values determine your emotions, and the energy created by emotions (emotional energy) in turn produces great performance. The trouble is, emotional energy can be positive or negative. Positive emotional energy produces memorable great performance whereas negative emotional energy produces regrettable performance and behavior. Great leaders understand the importance of recognizing and channeling their emotions toward great performance and away from regrettable performance. They also understand that a prerequisite to managing emotions is having clarity about values.

So how exactly do values determine emotions? A core trigger of emotions in life is either a match or a mismatch between deeply held values and the situation at hand. The degree and type of emotion felt depends on the extent of the match or mismatch. For example, if you value fairness and equality for all beings regardless of color or creed, you will experience anger and anxiety when faced with a situation that is unfair or discriminatory. On the other hand, you will experience happiness and joy when the situation at hand exemplifies equal treatment.

The human brain processes information roughly as follows: Each stimulus enters the brain from the back of the head near the brain stem. For it (the stimulus) to be processed logically, it must travel all the way to the front of the brain—to the neocortex. The neocortex is the home of logical processing. However, before a stimulus gets to the neocortex, it passes through another part of the brain called the amygdala, which is the home of emotions and feelings. When the brain experiences an emotion, the amygdala secretes adrenaline, which in turn produces the energy to act. The stronger the emotion, the greater the secretion of adrenaline. At this point there are two options available to the individual: one, use the energy positively toward something constructive, or two, let the secretion go unchecked until it completely clouds up the neocortex. In the latter case, the emotional brain (the amygdala) takes command and makes on-the-spot decisions about what to do and how to behave. Such an arrangement worked well until a few thousand years ago, when we were primitive beings. When one was faced with danger (a bigger, stronger animal) in the jungle, the amygdala helped decide if one should stay and fight or run for cover. In today's context, however, the amygdala can cause havoc.

When the amygdala takes control, many smart people do dumb things they later regret. If you have ever responded to an e-mail in anger and later regretted having done so, chances are your amygdala took control of the brain. Daniel Goleman, in his best-selling book *Emotional Intelligence*, refers to this phenomenon as "amygdala hijack." In short, the amygdala secretes adrenaline, and produces energy that enables strong action, which can be both positive and negative.

So what can one do about amygdala hijacks? As explained above, emotions happen when there is a match or mismatch between your deeply held values and the situation at hand. The only way to redirect negative energy during an amygdala hijack is to learn how to recognize your emotions as you experience them, and to understand what is triggering them. Once you have this clarity, over time, you can begin to recognize amygdala hijacks as they happen and redirect your impulses toward positive and productive action.

Before we go on to discuss the three questions that help define values, while we are on the subject of the brain, here is another feature of the brain to bear in mind. Unlike most other systems in the human body, according to Daniel Goleman the brain has an "open-loop" design. Most other systems, like the blood circulatory system, have closed-loop designs. A closed-loop design is one that does not interact with the same system of another human being. If you meet a person with abnormal blood pressure, because of the closed-loop design of the blood circulatory system, the other person's abnormal blood circulation has no impact on yours. However, because the brain is an open-loop system, your emotions impact people around you. When you hear someone saying, "Your enthusiasm is contagious," what they are really saying is that because of the open-loop design of the human brain, your emotions are transferring to their brain and they are feeling enthusiastic, too. Similarly, when at work a senior person walks the floors feeling stressed, the tension trickles down the floor.

Andrew, a senior professional in the retail wealth-management business, told me this story. His team conducted an interesting experiment. They asked branch managers to close their office doors and stay inside for a whole day as if they were in confidential meetings. Managers were also asked to pretend that they were discussing some serious and confidential issues. In an otherwise "open-door" culture, it was unusual for branch managers to be in closed-door meetings for a whole day. People could see through glass walls that managers were constantly on conference calls and looked very serious. The result of this action on the part of the branch manager was incredible. Commissions for the day for the entire office were down roughly 25 percent. Why? Because people stopped calling on clients to sell them trading ideas, and began to talk among themselves about why the manager's door was closed. Soon they began to fear the worst and wondered how safe their jobs were. According to Andrew, his team repeated this experiment in several branches and the result was the same.

Just as the open loop can transmit negative emotions as in the case above, the power of the open loop when it comes to motivating people should also be obvious. However, most people do not understand or appreciate this simple human phenomenon. Studies have shown that emotional energy is four times more powerful than rational energy. When faced with danger, humans are able to perform at levels not possible during normal conditions. This is because the emotion of fear produces huge amounts of adrenaline. When you leap in front of a car without bothering about your own safety to save your child from harm's way, your love is producing a great deal of adrenaline. Great leaders understand the power of emotion, and are able to harness it to motivate people to action. They do so by appealing to values. They consistently act according to a set of shared values, and those who "connect" with the values and behavior reward the leader with their devoted followership.

Let us now look at each of the three "values" questions in a bit of detail.

ow do I want people to experience me?

The first question to ask in defining your values is to think about how you want others to experience you. Imagine you've just taken over a new team. After spending the first day with you, how would you want the team to describe their new boss? If you could be a fly on the wall in a bar where they've collected for a beer after work, what would you like to hear them say when describing their first impressions of you? After they have worked with you for a few months, how would you like them to describe you? How would you like your family to describe you? Your friends?

One of the most powerful developmental experiences I have been through was called "Personal Best." People working closely with me were asked to describe how I behaved when at my personal best. The exercise deliberately did not ask about my negative behaviors or my weaknesses because the whole idea was to help me recognize my positive behaviors and get me to exhibit them more often. I looked at the data and asked myself why I didn't behave like this all the time. If I am capable of earning such praise, why can't I do this all the time? Careful reflection helped me recognize when my emotions produced negative impulses that prevented me from being at my personal best. I cannot say that I have fully mastered the art of redirecting all disruptive impulses, but as a result of consistent reflection, I am much better at it compared to earlier.

Asking yourself the question about how you want others to experience you begins to define what is important to you. If you want people to describe you as honest and sincere above all else, chances are you will act accordingly. If achievement and results orientation is what you want people to notice, then that is what will guide your behavior. When I asked Jacqueline Novogratz what her values were and how she wanted others to experience her, she was, as usual, completely clear. "I think about values at two levels. At the overarching level are two seemingly opposing ideas—audacity and humility. You have to have both at the same time. You need audacity to dream big, and the humility to keep your feet on the ground and be realistic. And below this overarching frame, I strongly believe in generosity, accountability, listening, leadership, integrity, and innovation. Those are both my personal values, and the values we are trying to inculcate in the culture at Acumen." The key point about question 4 is this: The more you think about how you want to portray yourself, the clearer you get about your values.

5. What values will guide my behavior?

By getting clear on how you want people to experience you, you have already begun to shed light on the values you choose to live by. For example, if you want people to think of you as an extremely hardworking and sincere person, you are acknowledging the fact that diligence and sincerity are important values for you. If they are not, chances are people will not experience you in this way. In this sense, question 5 either validates what you come up with in question 4 or forces you to go back and revisit your responses.

Great leaders not only have clarity about their values, they also have the courage to act according to them. Because they are challenging the status quo and envisioning a different future, their values-based behavior often makes them unpopular. A leader I worked for always emphasized "living the values" as a means to succeed at the company. He often reminded us that just making the numbers wasn't enough, and that to maximize our success as a team we needed to do both—make the numbers *and* live the values. His resolve was tested when one of the highest revenue producers on our team failed to improve his bad behavior with colleagues despite repeated feedback and warnings. Our leader decided to fire the "star producer" but ran into trouble because the division head (his boss) was dead set against it. The company did not want to lose such a great performer to competition. However, despite high personal risk, my leader let this star go. Knowing fully that our performance in the market would take an immediate dip, he gave a personal assurance to his superiors that he would make sure the team did well for the year as a whole. We did.

And from then onward, everyone got the message about the importance of living the values.

Before accepting a leadership position, bosses need to ask themselves if they are prepared to act according to their values. Most people succeed in life because they are rewarded for conforming and complying with the accepted norms of the culture in which they live and work. Leadership calls for challenging accepted norms. It is not a comfortable pursuit. Those who go into it with full knowledge of what is involved find the emotional and physical energy within them to face up to the challenges. That is leadership! No one can teach it to you—you have to discover and define it for yourself. And the only way to discover what leadership means for you is to honestly keep looking for answers to these questions until you find them.

Coming back to Gandhi again, he valued nonviolence above everything else. When he proposed nonviolent means of protesting against injustice, many were angered by his ideology and wanted to use violence against violence. However, Gandhi showed tremendous courage and acted in accordance with his values. Early in his struggle against discrimination in South Africa, he decided to challenge the government's rule requiring all colored people to carry an identification pass at all times. He questioned why only colored people were required to carry the passes and were punished if they failed to produce them when randomly checked by the police. To send this message to the authorities, he collected a group of people at a public place and spoke about the injustice. He then lit a small fire and burned his own pass, asking others to follow him. As the first few people burned their passes, the police warned them not to do so because the passes were government property. Gandhi disobeyed the police officer and continued to burn passes that were littered around the fire. After a couple of warnings, a police officer hit Gandhi with a baton with full force. Without retaliating, Gandhi continued to burn passes. The police officer struck again, but Gandhi continued to burn the passes even though he was bleeding profusely by then. Finally, the police officer struck Gandhi on his head, but Gandhi did not give up trying to burn another pass.

With trembling hands, he crawled toward another pass on the floor in an attempt to pick it up and throw it into the fire. The police officer lifted his baton yet again, but before striking Gandhi, he looked down and begged him to stop. "Don't make me continue to hit you while you don't retaliate at all . . ." he began to say, but could not complete his sentence as Gandhi had lost consciousness by then. The next day, the incident was all over the news media. Gandhi had succeeded in showing the world that there was another way to fight injustice—the nonviolent way—but it required courage equal to if not greater than the traditional violent way.

Here is another excellent example of leading with values, this time in a business setting. Several years ago I worked for a man I'll call Henry. When I think about the best leaders I have worked for thus far in my career, he always comes to mind as one of the finest. Almost everyone who worked for him would agree that it was energizing to be a part of the team. He was totally clear about his purpose and the basic principles (values) with which to achieve that purpose. Thanks to his strong belief and conviction about his purpose and values, he approached his work with a huge amount of enthusiasm and spent a lot of his time energizing others around him. When you heard him talk about his vision (*our* vision—he hardly ever used the word "I"—it was always "we" or "us") it was hard not to get excited. We wanted to do our best work for him. His (our) purpose was simple—to build the best client franchise on the street in the equities business, and to maximize revenue and profitability. He wanted our group to be the most trusted franchise in the equities business, and wanted us to make the maximum possible money at the same time. One principle he taught us, and reminded us of every day, was what he called "long-term greedy." The idea behind long-term greedy was simple but powerful. He wanted us to be hungry for client business, and wanted us to fight for every piece of business like there was no tomorrow. However, while doing so, we were always to keep the client's best interest in mind. By always acting in the client's best interest, we might occasionally lose in the short term, but would always win over the long term.

Henry insisted that we never stop thinking about what is right or wrong for the client. We should bid for a piece of business only if we were convinced that it was in the best long-term interest of the client. If it was not, we were to advise the client against doing the trade or transaction even if it meant the client could take his business to a competitor. In the "here and now" world of Wall Street, this is not an easy thing to do. Most people talk about being client-centric, but few are able to walk away from a lucrative deal, particularly when the client is asking for it.

As you can imagine, there were several occasions when we were faced with the dilemma of a client insisting on doing a transaction with us when in our assessment it would not be wise for him to do so. If we just executed the client's order without asking any questions, we stood to make huge fees instantly. If we tried to persuade the client to wait for a better time or not do the deal at all, we risked losing the business and the lucrative fees. In the short term—quarter to quarter—walking away from business is tough. Henry, however, was convinced that it was the right thing to do, and insisted that in the long run, clients would trust us more and we would win more business. We were often criticized for "losing" business, and the pressure to produce more and more revenue was tremendous. But Henry never wavered from his principle, and came down hard on anyone who violated it. He had the courage to stand up to a lot of opposition, and was not afraid of making himself unpopular in the short term. He did suffer occasionally in terms of his own performance bonuses, but over time had a very successful career at the firm. In fact, he was one of the youngest people to make partner. He later went on to become CEO of another firm and continues to guide his business in accordance with the "long-term greedy" principle.

The very essence of leadership is the ability to stay the course despite stiff opposition, because leaders succeed in spite of, not because of, their environment. Articulating a set of core values is only the first step. Behaving in accordance with stated values is the key. Real leaders differentiate themselves by their actions, not their words. The work of leadership involves taking personal hits, but having the courage to stay the course until you reach a tipping point when a sizable number of people begin to believe in your vision for a better future.

Before I conclude the discussion of this question, here is a word of caution. There is a very thin line between sticking to your purpose and values and being stubborn. While leaders must be prepared to act according to their values, and be ready to be in the game for the long haul, they must also keep an open mind and be prepared to change their views as they receive new information. It is this fine balancing act that makes leadership more an art than a science.

6. What situations cause me to feel strong emotions?

The last question attempts to build your self-awareness. Over two decades of running leadership development programs, I have found that while people think they are very self-aware, they are actually not. If you ask someone, "Do you know yourself well?" the intuitive answer is "yes, of course." However, if you follow that up with questions like "What is your purpose?," "What are your deeply held values?," or "When and why do you feel strong emotions?," they start struggling for clear answers. As stated earlier, there is a strong link between emotions and performance. High performance is a function of emotional energy. In order to understand what gives you emotional energy, you need to be able to understand your emotions. To understand and recognize your emotions, you need to know your values. Now that you have clarified your values, it is time to better understand situations that cause you to feel emotions. Once you are aware of situations that cause you to feel emotions, you have more control over your behavior the next time you feel the same emotion. This is because you can now recognize an amygdala hijack in the making, and prevent it from happening.

Many situations aggravate us during the normal course of a business day. If we do and say exactly as we feel in every instance, we will find it really hard to keep a job or keep friends. With fuller clarity about values and emotions, it becomes easier to control your actions and focus your energy on only the most important things—those that will make a material difference toward achieving your purpose.

To summarize, in order to create a better future leaders need energy in abundance. Clarity about purpose and values is the only lasting source of leadership energy. Leadership is a choice, not a promotion, position, or title. To promote yourself to being a leader, start with the six questions. Besides giving you a strong leadership foundation, they will also help you navigate through difficult times.

To be sure, there will be stressful times in your work and personal life when you will not know what to do. From time to time, the best of us get frozen, and start behaving in unproductive ways because we allow the tough environment to get the better of us. Resilience—the ability to unfreeze oneself from such situations and move forward decisively—is critical both to getting ahead in business and to being a good leader.

Many years ago when I worked for a large company division, my boss, with whom I had a great relationship, suddenly left the company. Even though almost everything we did was related to employee development, my division was not a part of Human Resources; it was an independent function. Since it was not immediately obvious to whom I should report upon my boss's sudden departure, they had me report to two people, one of whom was the head of Human Resources. Unfortunately for me, there was a severe, unhealthy rivalry between my old and new bosses. As is common in many organizations, the rivalry was a result of a flawed organizational structure—one that had our division "compete" with the departments headed by my two new bosses. Under my old boss's leadership, my division had grown in prominence and we had celebrated many successes in the previous three years, often to the annoyance of my new bosses. It soon became clear to me that things would never be the same again. Not only were my new bosses keen on undoing a lot of what we had put in place over the past three years, but I was never going to have the support I had from my old boss.

Being an executive officer of the company, my old boss was privy to all the important information, and ensured his staff's inclusion in key company-wide initiatives. He was a great champion for our work, and our success was in no small part due to his support. All this began to change and I found myself becoming isolated. During the first four months of this "regime change," I spent most of my time defending what we had done in the past, while my team did not get a chance to work on any new high-profile assignments. I began to realize that this situation would lead to an unhappy ending, but did not know what to do to avoid it. I started networking with headhunters and other industry contacts, and felt the need to stay close to my computer and phone so that I could be on top of any information that might be helpful. As a result I started to spend a lot more time in my office with the door closed. I came to dread my own staff meetings because my people would ask me questions such as "What is the future of our division?" or "Will they downsize us and will we now be at the mercy of HR?"—questions for which I had no answers.

Because of my close relationship with my previous boss, I had free access to the CEO and to the executive floor. This allowed me to "be in the know" when important things were unfolding within any of our businesses, and allowed me to offer talent-management expertise to senior leaders as they grew their businesses. In this sense, we had a lot of "deal flow"—opportunities to work on high-profile initiatives. My people had come to expect a lot of deal flow from me, and could not understand why that was not the case anymore. As the weeks rolled by, I began to feel more and more uncomfortable but had no idea how to proceed. I silently wished that someone very senior would realize this huge mistake and separate my division into an independent function again, thereby freeing me from my new managers. It was only a matter of time, I thought, before things would look up again.

Does my situation sound familiar? What I was experiencing during this time is what I call temporary "freezing"; I had frozen in the face of unexpected turbulence. Unfortunately, this happens to the best of us, and it happens several times in one's career. Furthermore, many successful executives never come out of their frozen state even though they have been very successful until that point. The temporary freezing becomes permanent and their careers begin to derail. Those who have the resilience to unfreeze themselves are able to do so because of a high level of self-awareness driven by their clarity of purpose and values. First, they accept reality and come to an honest assessment of how bad the situation really is. They do so by assessing the importance of the situation in the context of their overall purpose. If it is indeed critical to overall purpose, they make a decision to snap out of their frozen state and decide to do something about it. Finally, their values give them clues about how to navigate out of the situation. The important point here is not how to find solutions, but to *decide* that you *do* want to find them. The key is to change your mind state from reactive to proactive—from being a victim to being in charge. People with clarity of purpose and values are able to do this much better than those without such clarity. They do this by asking themselves two questions: 1) How important is this issue in the overall scheme of things for me?, and 2) If I were to act according to my values, how would I change my behavior in order to solve the problem?

Fortunately for me, I was able to navigate the situation successfully. I explained my situation to a friend and professional colleague and asked her for advice. After listening carefully while probing to make sure I had told her everything, she asked me, "What if a coaching client of yours shared this exact story with you and asked for your advice? How would you help your client?" It did not take me long to answer. "I would ask my client what his overall purpose was—the key mission he was working on—and follow up by asking how the current crisis was affecting the mission," I said without hesitation. "I would then probe to find out if my client had fully accepted reality, and try to get him to take control again by looking at just one thing he could do to influence the situation."

Prompted by my friend, I began to see myself in my situation. I realized I was "frozen," and was going deeper and deeper into my own self-created misery without doing anything about it. I also realized that I needed to stop feeling sorry for myself and to stop blaming my new masters for my troubles. I had to come to grips with the fact that my world had changed forever, and that I now needed to operate differently. I also reminded myself that my key mission—my purpose—had not changed. I still wanted to create the most sustainable competitive advantage for my company: a powerful leadership development engine to create the best leaders at all levels. Clarity about my values helped me recognize my own emotions. Once I took charge of my emotions, the clarity of my purpose helped me formulate a plan, which was simply to sit down with my new bosses and seek their input about what would be a new vision for our division. As I began talking to them at a very different (forward-looking) level, I learned that their biggest problem in the past had been that my old boss did not give them a chance to express their views. They were feeling unheard. Soon I built a trust-based relationship with my new bosses and we began working well together.

As a coach, I have seen many extremely successful executives freezing just like I had frozen. Many were not able to recover. Those who did followed the same steps I did. They:

1. Accepted reality (stopped living in denial)

2. Reminded themselves of their core purpose and values in order to reenergize themselves

3. Changed their state of mind from victim to in charge

4. Were prepared to change their own behavior

HOWARD SCHULTZ:
A JOURNEY OF SELF-DISCOVERY

Pick any leader you admire and chances are you will find that he or she was very clear about the six questions. One who particularly stands out for me is Howard Schultz, chairman and CEO of Starbucks. Since he became CEO in 1987, Starbucks has grown from a small local company with six stores and fewer than a hundred employees to an international brand with more than sixteen thousand stores in over fifty countries. More remarkable than its spectacular growth is the fact that it is a company built on values and guiding principles seldom seen in the corporate world. It has proven that a company can lead with its values (in this case, treating its people with respect and dignity) and still make money. The retail industry is known for its high employee churn and use of temporary workers. This helps companies keep costs low and avoid benefits' costs. Starbucks, on the other hand, became the first American company to provide health-care benefits to part-time employees, and is highly profitable despite the fact that it spends more money on benefits than on buying coffee.

Fascinated by what Starbucks stood for, I decided to find out more. As I researched and read more about Howard Schultz's journey, I realized what a remarkable story of leadership it was. Schultz grew up in government-subsidized housing in Brooklyn, New York. His father never earned more than $20,000 a year. He was seven when his father, a temporary truck driver, broke his leg and was stuck at home for a month without income, health insurance, or workers' compensation. He often heard his parents talk about their monetary situation, and who else they could borrow from to make ends meet. His mother would sometimes have him take calls from bill collectors and instruct him to tell them his parents were not home. Schultz could not understand why his father's company would not help them at a time like this, particularly when the accident had occurred at work. His values began to take shape at that early stage. He knew then that if he were ever in a position to make a difference, he would never treat people in the way that his father's company had.

A natural athlete, Schultz went to Northern Michigan University on an athletic scholarship; given his family's finances, it was perhaps the only way he could have done so. After college, he got a job with Xerox Corp. in the sales training program. There he learned skills that would remain with him for life—selling, marketing, presenting, and cold-calling. Success came early, and he sold more machines than most of his peers over the next three years. He rented an apartment in Greenwich Village, and was clearly on a roll. The only problem was that he never developed a passion for copy machines; he soon began to feel antsy and craved a new challenge. In 1979 he learned about a Swedish company, Perstorp, that was planning to set up a U.S. subsidiary for its Hammerplast line of houseware products, and joined them in North Carolina to sell components for kitchens and furniture. Soon promoted to vice president and general manager of Hammerplast, he returned to New York and started overseeing all U.S. operations, managing about twenty sales reps. At twenty-eight, he had clearly arrived. With a $75,000 salary, a company car, and an expense account, he bought an apartment on the Upper East Side and moved in with the love of his life.

His parents could hardly believe the life he was living just six years out of college, and could never understand why he began to feel restless again. While life was good by any standards, he hadn't found his purpose yet. He still did not know where and how he would find it, but longed to control his own destiny. Something—passion—was missing. It wasn't until he came up with the idea of creating the Starbucks chain of stores that he realized what it means to work on something that fully captures the heart and the imagination.

He came across the idea purely by chance. While still at Hammerplast, he noticed a small retailer was placing unusually large orders for a manual drip coffeemaker, and decided to investigate. He was curious to know why Starbucks Coffee, Tea and Spice in Seattle, Washington, was buying this simple device in such quantities, and flew over to meet with the owners and find out.

Life would never be the same for Schultz from the day he landed in Seattle for the first time. He found out that the people of Starbucks, then a small company with only four stores selling roasted coffee beans, were passionate about their product. They recommended manual coffee brewing because with electric coffeemakers, the coffee sits around and gets burned. In his book, *Pour Your Heart into It,* Schultz recalls that from the moment he drank his first freshly brewed Starbucks espresso he was hooked. "We don't manage the business to maximize anything except the quality of the coffee," the founder of Starbucks told him. After touring the roasting plant and spending some time learning about the whole process of buying, roasting, and selling quality coffee, he was totally enamored, and decided that he wanted to live in Seattle and work for Starbucks. An important point to note is that at this time Starbucks only sold coffee beans, and was not in the coffee-brewing and café business.

On the flight back to New York the next day, Schultz could not stop thinking about Starbucks. There was something magical about the coffee culture, and he began to dream about being a part of the magic. "Maybe I can help grow it," he thought, and wondered if the owners would be willing to hire him and even give him a small equity stake. By the time the plane landed, Schultz had begun to shape his purpose, and began a yearlong journey to convince the owners to hire him.

If he were to succeed in his mission of joining Starbucks, it would mean taking a serious pay cut, saying good-bye to the prestige of a job in a multinational corporation, and moving three thousand miles away from New York to a tiny coffee company. It did not make sense to anyone, but as the months rolled by, Schultz became more and more convinced that growing Starbucks was what he wanted to do. He could see endless possibilities. Starbucks could become a nationwide business with hundreds of stores. When the owners finally invited him to discuss the idea of his joining the company, and the possibility of growing it into a much bigger business, Schultz thought he had impressed them enough and would definitely get an offer. So he could hardly believe his ears when they told him they had decided against it and would not hire him. He saw his entire future crash and burn even before it had taken off.

But even after the "rejection," he could not get Starbucks off his mind. He wasn't going to accept no for an answer, and called the owners back the next day to plead his case. The owners reconsidered their position after hearing him out, agreed that he was right, and invited him to join the company. Had he not called them again, he would not have joined Starbucks, and the rest would not be history. How did he have the courage and perseverance to keep pushing even while friends and family were advising him to stay with the safer route in New York? This is the courage of conviction that comes with clarity of purpose. In fact, such courage cannot be found without clarity of purpose.

A little over a year into his life at Starbucks, Schultz was sent to Milan, Italy, to attend an international housewares show. While walking to the trade show on his first morning in Milan, he noticed a small espresso bar and walked in. He watched the man behind the counter make an espresso and a cappuccino for the two customers in front of him, and asked for an espresso for himself. Half a block later, he noticed another espresso bar, and another two in the next few blocks. It was on that day in Milan that he understood what he calls the romance of coffee bars in Italy. It occurred to him that Starbucks was in the wrong business. Besides selling high-quality coffee beans, it needed to sell freshly brewed coffee in coffee bars just like in Italy. The thought of coffee bars all across America was so powerful that he recalls he started shaking. Now his purpose was fully shaped.

Unfortunately, his partners were not impressed with his idea. They wanted to remain coffee-bean retailers and did not want to get into the restaurant or bar business. Doing so would take them away from the core mission of the company, they argued. Not unlike when he was trying to convince them to hire him, it took nearly a year of persistence for Schultz to bring them around to agree to test the idea. They agreed to give him three hundred square feet (he had asked for fifteen hundred) to set up a counter to try out his experiment at one of the stores. The idea was a runaway hit from the first day. The store became a gathering place, and week after week, business continued to grow. Schultz could feel the possibilities deep within his guts, and was convinced that any doubts his partners had about expanding into the brewed coffee business should have disappeared by this point, and that they would readily approve expansion. However, he could not have been more wrong, because the whole success of the experiment seemed wrong to his partners and they had no desire to dilute the original mission of their company. When he realized he could not convince them to move in the direction he believed so deeply in, he decided to leave the company and start one of his own, in which he could pursue his vision. As fate would have it, just as he was making up his mind, he found out that his wife was pregnant. Would it be wise to quit a secure job at Starbucks and live without a salary at a time like this? In Schultz's mind, there was never any question about doing anything else. By now, he was absolutely clear about the results he wanted to create.

While he was raising the money needed to start Il Giornale, his new company, people gave him every reason why his idea would never work. Not only were they unwilling to invest, many were rude and disrespectful. From "How could you leave Starbucks?" to "You're out of your mind. This is insane. You should just go get a job," he heard every possible insult. Of the 242 people he approached to raise capital, 217 said no. Yet he never gave up his strong belief in the future he saw in his idea, and ultimately raised enough money from the rest to get Il Giornale off the ground.

From the moment the first store opened for customers, sales exceeded expectations. By the end of the first year, business had grown steadily and the company had three stores. At this time, the owners of Starbucks unexpectedly decided to sell their company. While Schultz had just gone through a marathon fund-raising exercise for his small company, he knew instantly that he needed to buy Starbucks. Again, with very little money of his own, he started out and eventually managed to convince investors to give him the $4 million needed. By August 1987, the acquisition was completed, and the combined company was renamed Starbucks. At thirty-four, Howard Schultz, the young boy from the Brooklyn projects, had the opportunity to create America's biggest coffee company. More importantly, he would create a company that would put treating its people with respect and dignity above all else. It would be the kind of company his father never had the chance to work for. In all my years of researching business leadership, I have not come across a story that better exemplifies the central ideas of this chapter:

- Before you can lead others successfully, you need to lead yourself.

- Self-leadership is having limitless energy to stay the course in the face of the most formidable of obstacles.

- The only two permanent sources of limitless personal energy are purpose and values.

2

ENLIST Co-Leaders: Team Leadership

As I walked into the auditorium at Morgan Stanley headquarters on Thursday, September 18, 2008, to attend a town hall meeting and hear from CEO John Mack, the air was tense. Over the previous weekend, two of the most storied U.S. investment banks had ceased to exist as the world had known them. Lehman Brothers had declared bankruptcy, and Bank of America had bought Merrill Lynch. Earlier that year, Bear Stearns had been sold for almost nothing to JPMorgan Chase. Not only had so many friends lost their jobs at Lehman and Bear, they had lost much of their savings as well. Like most of my colleagues, I was worried and uncertain about the future. None of us had seen anything quite like this before. To make matters worse, no one felt sorry for bankers. If anything, we were seen as criminals who deserved what was happening to us.

Through all of the previous week, television crews had camped outside Lehman Brothers headquarters on Seventh Avenue in New York, diagonally across the block from us. Soon after the story about Lehman's bankruptcy broke on Sunday night, the TV crews, instead of packing up, simply turned around and trained their lenses on our building. News channels like CNBC were repeatedly raising the question Will Morgan Stanley make it? In fact, a news reporter stopped me while I was walking out of the office building and asked if I would comment on the mood inside the building. I remember feeling irritated and angry with him, and walked away without responding. Our stock, which had been at $43.27 just a week before, was in free fall, and had already dropped to the teens by the time John Mack took the stage that morning. Even a decision to accelerate the announcement of blowout quarterly earnings earlier that week did nothing to halt the free fall. We started the week with over $180 billion in cash, and announced excellent earnings, with a healthy 16.2 percent return on equity, but nothing seemed to matter, and the stock continued to slide.

John looked tired after having spent the past few days and nights in the office. Despite the clear signs of fatigue, he seemed, as always, in control. For the third time that week, he was about to address all employees globally via video link. He started the broadcast with "I know some of you are worried. These are unprecedented times, and the first thing I want to say to you is this, if you want to sell your stock, sell it. I am not keeping a list of who sells and who holds, do what makes you comfortable. I can tell you that I am not selling, but if you want to do so, do it." He then went on to give as much information as he possibly could about what was going on in the market. He explained that we were in the midst of a market controlled by fear and rumors, and that short sellers were driving our stock down. To fully understand the gravity of the situation, it is important to understand what was going on in the market at that time. After Lehman and Merrill had perished, at 2:45 p.m. every day, hedge-fund managers would demand to draw their entire credit and margin balances, short Morgan Stanley's stock, and buy credit default swaps (CDS) at the same time. This was akin to buying a life insurance policy on someone, then doing everything possible to accelerate their death. By shorting the stock, fund managers were betting that the stock would go down. By buying credit default swaps, they were driving the cost of insuring Morgan Stanley's debt higher. When the cost of insuring debt inches higher, the market sees it as a sign of weakness and drives the stock down. When the stock does go down because of the increasing cost of debt insurance, the original short sellers can cover their short positions and make a tidy profit. This was the position Morgan Stanley found itself in.

Money was steadily going out the door, and the firm faced a definite possibility of running out of cash—a classic run on the bank, and exactly what had happened to Lehman the previous week. As the CDS spreads continued to widen, Morgan Stanley's clearing bankers (like JPMorgan, Credit Suisse) demanded more collateral to continue business with them. To make matters worse, some of the people who were driving the stock into the ground were the firm's own clients.

Morgan Stanley and Goldman Sachs were the only two independent U.S. investment banks left. To say that the collapse of Morgan Stanley would cause serious ramifications to the entire global financial system would be an understatement. If Morgan Stanley went down, Goldman, and several other global (main street) corporations, would probably not be far behind. This fact was not lost on regulators, and they were keen to find a way to avoid such a catastrophe. It was clear that for Morgan Stanley to survive, it either needed a fresh infusion of capital or had to merge with a larger bank. Treasury Secretary Hank Paulson, Chairman of the Federal Reserve Ben Bernanke, and President of the New York Federal Reserve Tim Geithner were urging John Mack to find a solution.

Unless something changed dramatically, Morgan Stanley would be the next in line after Lehman and Merrill. We were on the brink of death, but came through alive and mostly unharmed thanks largely to the way John and his top team managed the crisis.

A year after that fateful month, I sat down with John Mack and he explained the situation as follows: "On the Friday before Lehman's collapse, we [my CFO and I], along with other bank CEOs, were invited to a meeting at the New York Fed to discuss a private solution to save Lehman. It was clear that after what had happened to Fannie Mae and Freddie Mac, Secretary Paulson did not have the political capital in Washington to arrange another bailout. They [Paulson, Bernanke, and

Geithner] wanted us to collectively come up with enough capital to create a 'bad bank' to house Lehman's low-quality assets. Even though we were uncomfortable with the idea, we clearly needed to do something about it as an industry. But the conversation centered around the fact that even if we could do this, what would we do if AIG goes under, and if Merrill goes under? It was much bigger than Lehman. Everything was discussed very openly, but the meeting ended without an agreement." (Note: By asking to create a "bad bank," they were essentially asking the banking industry to contribute capital into a joint venture of sorts that would buy off the bad assets from Lehman. This would take pressure off Lehman and it would survive. The logic was that the survival of Lehman was good for the industry as a whole.)

Over the weekend when Lehman collapsed and Merrill Lynch was sold, it was clear to John that Morgan Stanley would be next. Goldman Sachs was feeling the same pressures at this time, though to a lesser extent, because the next in line was Morgan Stanley. "Lloyd Blankfein [CEO of Goldman] kept telling me, John, you've got to hold on because I am just twenty seconds behind you," said Mack while describing the events of the week. While John and his team were working round the clock through the crisis to find a capital infusion, Tim Geithner called insisting to know what was the firm's "Plan B." By Friday, Mack and team had already spoken with Citigroup, JPMorgan, Wachovia, and the Chinese fund CIC about infusing capital or doing a merger. Nobody wanted to do a deal that was anywhere close to fair. Even as the top team at Morgan Stanley was on the brink of breaking with fatigue and stress, Tim Geithner continued to insist on learning about Plan B. Eventually, on Friday afternoon a ray of hope emerged—the Japanese banking giant Mitsubishi UFJ Financial Group was interested in investing in Morgan Stanley, and wanted to talk at 5 p.m. on Sunday.

On Sunday morning, while the top team was in the office preparing for negotiations with the Japanese, John received a call from Paulson, Bernanke, and Geithner. He recounted the whole conversation: "They said to me that they were extremely worried about a global economic meltdown, and did not want chaos in the market on Monday morning.

They wanted us to do something with our firm before markets opened on Monday. Ben Bernanke said, we see things you don't see, this is bigger than just one firm, it is a global crisis, and we need you to do something. Tim Geithner, who had been persistent all along about Plan B, then adds, "Call Jamie [Dimon] at JPMorgan, he'll buy your bank." When John told them he had already spoken to Jamie and that he did not want to buy the firm, Geithner insisted that if John called him back, Jamie would buy the firm. What Geithner did not say, however, was that Jamie would be willing to buy the firm perhaps at a dollar a share.

"When I heard that, I said to the three of them," recounts Mack, "'Let me ask you a question: I have forty-five thousand employees. In New York City, you have AIG, Lehman Brothers, Bear Stearns, Merrill Lynch, and the other layoffs—probably forty thousand jobs have already been lost. From a public policy standpoint, does this [merging Morgan Stanley with JPMorgan Chase] make sense?'" Tim Geithner responded by saying it was not about public policy. Instead it was about financial stability, and that they needed Mack to do something about his firm. "I took a deep breath and said calmly," he continued, "'I have the utmost respect for the three of you. What you do for this country makes you patriots. But I have forty-five thousand employees. I will not do it. Thank you.'"

I don't need to emphasize how much courage, conviction, and focus were required of John Mack and his team during this time. Not only did they have the responsibility of saving the firm, they had all the pressure from the regulators to do something (i.e., go down) in the larger interest of market stability. Ultimately, the firm was successful in securing a $9 billion investment from Mitsubishi, and survived. At the time of this writing, eighteen months have passed since that fateful week. Morgan Stanley has a new CEO while John Mack is still chairman, and the firm is on solid ground.

I asked John how he found the will to fight the fight, and he told me he had no choice. He found his firm under attack, thought about the future of forty-five thousand employees, and knew instantly that he had to do everything in his power to save it. "Anyone in my position would have done the same thing. When you are that close to death, you are totally focused on one thing—survival. I had no fear of the three regulators. They were doing their job and I had to do mine. The team around me was superb. Together we made it. We survived," he said softly. I am not sure how many others in John's shoes would have made the call Mack made. What made him do it? It was his clarity of purpose and his values which told him to focus on his employees' needs.

During my years at Morgan Stanley, I watched John closely. I had already worked with several CEOs and senior leaders before coming to Morgan Stanley. While I was working with John, it became abundantly clear to me that one of his biggest strengths was the way he managed his immediate team of direct reports. They were fiercely loyal to him. Unrelated to the crisis of 2008, I asked him what aspects of running the firm he generally focuses his own efforts on the most, and he was quick to say, "The most important thing for me as CEO is to support my team. I try to be there for them. When they need coaching, I coach them. When they need any other type of support, I do the best I can. My main job is to support my team." This was evident even during the crisis. Not only did he do a stupendous job of keeping his own emotions in check (there was no shortage of stories about captains of the financial industry cracking under pressure that month), he stayed focused on supporting the team.

Being a leader means energizing and motivating your team of direct reports to perform at a higher level. Again, there is no shortage of literature and advice on this issue, yet more managers get it wrong than right. There is no doubt that a motivated and energized workforce translates directly into a better bottom line. Furthermore, most managers want to keep their people motivated. The problem is that in the clamor of all the advice on how best to motivate their people, managers don't even know where to begin. Sometimes I think we are so poor at motivating people *because* there is so much information on how to do it. Most of it is too complex. Another factor is that today's managers generally tend to be player-coaches, meaning that they have individual production responsibilities in addition to their managerial roles. Who has the time for all the "people issues"? If only there were a simple way of thinking about it. If only there were some tangible things managers could do without investing a ton of time. There are. Here's a one-minute course on energizing and motivating others:

1. However hard you try, you cannot motivate another human being. Humans are premotivated by their individual purpose and values.

2. Don't ask yourself what *you* can *do* to motivate them; try to find out how they are already motivated.

3. Once you know their personal motivation triggers, try as best you can to match their expectations with the work at hand. For example, if someone enjoys creative work, give them more assignments involving creative work. If someone likes customer interface more than processing, try to give them opportunities to interact with customers. The point is, now that you know what they like, to the extent possible, design their job in a way that gives them an opportunity to do what they like best.

4. If, however, there is a complete mismatch between personal motivators and the work at hand, rather than fixing the problem with carrots or sticks, the best course is to find a better fit. In other words, if the demands of the job are diametrically opposite of what the individual is energized by, then it is best to help this individual find another job or role.

So the key is: You have to figure out what your people expect from their jobs, and do your best to link people's expectations with the work you want them to do. Your immediate reaction upon reading this probably is: "This is easier said than done. How do I even begin to find out what each of my direct reports wants?" Fortunately, it is far less daunting than most people think, because most employees care about the same three things in their professional life. When I tell people that everyone cares about the same three things, most initially disagree with me. After all, we're all different. But take a few minutes to try the following exercise before you continue reading the rest of this chapter.

Imagine you are about to change jobs and have two competing offers. Both jobs pay roughly the same amount of money and are in the same industry. Both are at reputable companies. How will you choose between the two jobs? What factors will you consider while making your decision?

What factors did you consider? Did you think about the exact nature of your role, and how your work will fit in with the larger picture of the organization? Did you consider your own strengths and limitations and think about which of the two will be better suited for you? Did you think about the work culture of the two organizations? Did you consider the quality of your coworkers, and the way they interact with each other? Did you consider the reputation of the companies? Did you think about future career prospects? Most people go through a list like that when making career decisions.

I have facilitated this exercise in my seminars with hundreds of executives around the world. I pose the same imaginary dilemma, and ask them to tell me what they are likely to consider while making a decision. As they begin to talk, I write down their responses on one of three blank flip charts in front of the room. Each flip chart represents one of the three things people care about, but while I facilitate this discussion and capture their responses, there are no titles on the flip charts. After capturing participants' responses on the three charts, I reveal the hidden titles, which are:

- ROLE

- ENVIRONMENT

- DEVELOPMENT

I then explain that most employees care about the same three things—the nature of their *R*ole, their work *E*nvironment, and their professional *D*evelopment *(RED).* I ask them if they agree with me that all of their responses fit in with one or more of the three RED buckets. I have yet to hear a response that does not belong in one of these three categories. Slowly it begins to dawn upon people that while each employee's preferences are unique, everyone cares about those three overarching things.

As managers, you need to talk regularly with employees about the three buckets, and as you keep the dialogue going, listen for information about their preferences and aspirations. Armed with this information, you can *label and link* day-to-day work with their expectations. For example, if you know that one of your employees wants to get more experience in dealing with cross-border transactions, you might staff her on a team that is working on an important transaction. However, before giving her that assignment, you must talk to her and tell her (label) that you are doing so because it will give her the experience she needs, and explain (link) that it will help her in her career progression if she gains cross-border expertise.

In my experience with managing people all over the world, I have found that most ineffective managers are considered ineffective not because they don't know *how* to motivate people, but because they don't know *what* motivates their people. This is an important distinction, and perhaps the biggest key to motivating others. Most managers think they know what motivates their direct reports, but when you ask them, they actually list things that motivate *them*. They falsely assume that what motivates them also motivates others. I have quizzed countless managers about their knowledge of their direct reports' motivation, and most fall short.

Granted that one person's preferences and expectations are different from the next, once you know what they are, it is relatively easy to meet the expectations. Most managers are able to meet employees' expectations in the normal course of day-to-day work without making any major concessions. If, however, there is a massive disconnect between an employee's expectations and the role, environment, and development features of the job, then in the long run it is best both for the employee and the organization to separate. Unfortunately, many employees are dissatisfied even when it is possible to match the RED features with their preferences, and this is so because managers don't even try to find out what the employees' preferences are. The key really is in keeping the dialogue going with your people.

You will find that it does not take a lot of time to energize people if you organize your interaction and communication with employees around the simple RED framework. All it takes is a bit of proactive action on the part of managers during the normal course of day-to-day functioning.

DEGREES OF ENGAGEMENT

As you read about these real features in more detail below, consider one more key point about employee motivation. Factors that energize and motivate someone and those that disengage someone are not the opposite of one another. In fact they are two different sets of factors. In other words, for me to be highly energized and engaged about something, a certain set of factors and conditions, such as alignment of the work with personal purpose and values, must be present. The absence of those factors and conditions does not mean I am disengaged or de-motivated. It is just that I am not operating at full energy. There is a totally different set of factors that disengage or de-motivate me. These are usually the absence of basic factors such as salary and working conditions, what are commonly called hygiene factors. There are three degrees of employee engagement: 1) dissatisfied and disengaged; 2) satisfied but not fully energized; and 3) fully energized and emotionally engaged.

At the bottom of the ladder the employee is *dissatisfied and dis-*

Hierarchy of Employee Engagement

ENERGIZED
In addition to basic hygiene factors, individual motivation triggers are activated. Employee is emotionally engaged and performance is at full potential.

SATISFIED BUT NOT ENERGIZED
Basic hygiene factors are satisfactory, but true emotional engagement is missing. Performance is adequate but not at full potential.

DISSATISFIED/DISENGAGED
The lack of basic hygiene factors such as salary, working conditions, relationship with manager, company policies, etc. are so disruptive that the employee would leave at the first available opportunity.

engaged. Here, basic factors such as salary, working conditions, relationships with manager and coworkers, and company policies are so unsatisfactory that the employee is ready to jump ship at the first decent opportunity. Productivity and performance are low.

At one step above dissatisfaction and disengagement, the employee is *satisfied but not energized.* As stated above, being energized is not the opposite of being dissatisfied and disengaged. In 1959, Frederick Herzberg—the noted psychologist—proposed the "Two-Factor Theory," according to which he argued that there are two distinct and unrelated sets of factors (hygiene factors and motivators) that lead to dissatisfaction and high motivation, and that the increase of one set does not automatically lead to the decrease in the other. Based on 203 interviews with accountants and engineers, he concluded that the nature of the work an employee performs has the capacity to gratify such needs as achievement, status, personal worth, and self-realization, thus making her happy and motivated. However, the absence of such gratifying job characteristics does not necessarily lead to unhappiness and dissatisfaction. Instead, dissatisfaction results from unfavorable assessments of such job-related factors as company policies, supervision, technical problems, salary, interpersonal relations on the job, and working conditions.

At the highest level of motivation, the employee is *emotionally engaged and energized*. In this state, she willingly goes the extra mile most of the time because she *wants to*. Performance is top-notch and the employee does her best possible work every day because hygiene factors are satisfactory and individual motivators are activated.

So what should leaders and managers do to get their direct reports emotionally engaged and energized? The first step is to turn this question around. Start not with thinking about how to make your employee better, and instead try to understand what your employees need to be emotionally engaged. Find out their expectations and their preferences about their role, environment, and development. Once you know better what your people expect, you will have a much better chance of meeting those needs. Let us look at each of the buckets more closely first, and come back to how to apply them to keeping people motivated and energized.

ROLE

At a macro level, most people like to work in an organization that has a compelling vision, and the vision must be accompanied by a compelling strategy. At a micro level, the role must provide adequate challenge, must fit meaningfully within the overall big picture, provide adequate freedom to do the job well, and must align with personal purpose and values. Let me highlight some of these elements a bit more.

VISION AND STRATEGY

Two construction workers on the same site were asked the same question: What are you doing? One said, "I am laying bricks," and the other said, "I am building a house." Which one was more energized about his work? Most employees want to work in a place that has a compelling vision for future success. So this is the first expectation under the "role" bucket: Does the organization have a vision that an employee can relate to? For someone to get on a bus willingly, the intended destination of the bus should be appealing to a traveler.

The next thing employees want to know is if there is an effective strategy to achieve the vision. Everyone likes to belong to a winning team, and winning teams usually have a strategy. Most people also want to have a say on strategy and enjoy being involved in setting the strategy. This is good news for managers and leaders; they need not shoulder the entire burden of strategy formulation by themselves. Some managers make the mistake of thinking that it is their duty to come up with a plan and provide very specific direction to their people. Instead, they should invite their team members to work together in formulating the strategy. We will discuss how to do this in a lot of detail in chapter 4.

CHALLENGING AND MEANINGFUL GOALS

Moving from the macro to the micro level, the next thing most employees want to ensure is that they have a challenging but achievable set of individual goals that support the overall strategy. They must understand how their own work fits into the vision and strategy. Most of us have a need to do meaningful work, and to be recognized and appreciated for it. Having specific goals and knowing how they fit into the big picture goes a long way toward meeting this need. Once they have a set of goals, most people want sufficient freedom to work on them.

FREEDOM AND AUTHORITY

Hardly anybody likes to be micromanaged. Not having the freedom to do their job well is a big source of job dissatisfaction. Marcus Buckingham and Curt Coffman, authors of *First, Break All the Rules,* suggest a simple recipe to achieve the right balance between freedom and oversight: Control the end and not the means. This means spending adequate time with your direct reports in agreeing upon specific outcomes you expect from them, then leaving them free to achieve them. Of course, you should make yourself available when they need help, but clear articulation and agreement on expected outcomes largely removes the need for micromanagement.

I was dissatisfied with the efforts of my marketing and business development team in one of my corporate roles. As time passed, I became restless and worried about results or the lack of them. My immediate temptation was to take control and start directly managing the group on a daily basis. Fortunately, I did not do that and instead called the head of the group to my office and had a discussion with him about my concerns. We agreed that he would do a business planning session with his entire team and show me detailed goals, objectives, deadlines, and outcomes for each market segment. He spent a whole day with his team and then showed me a very well-thought-out plan with specific outcomes. Not only did I get what I wanted, but the entire team felt energized because they felt ownership of the plan and were excited about their prospects. Over the next few months, their performance exceeded expectations. Micromanagement on my part would have demoralized the group and performance would not have been as spirited as it turned out to be.

ALIGNMENT WITH PURPOSE AND VALUES

Finally, and most importantly, most people like to play roles that align with their personal purpose and values. Most of us come to work with a desire to be successful. A role that does not give us an opportunity to achieve our personal purpose and live according to our values is unlikely to meet this need. When personal purpose and values are in alignment with organizational goals and values, people are energized to the fullest, and this energy translates into superior financial results. According to one study I saw a while ago, only 50 percent of surveyed U.S. employees said their professional careers gave them the most satisfaction in life, with "family" coming in closely behind at 40 percent. This means there is huge untapped energy that can be released if managers can do a better job of first selecting the right people, then aligning personal aspirations with organizational goals.

For an employee to be highly engaged and energized at work, he/she must strongly agree with the following six statements regarding his/her role:

- Our organization has a compelling vision for its future success.

- We have an effective/differentiated strategy to achieve the vision.

- I have challenging (stretch) but achievable goals.

- I clearly understand how my work fits into the overall vision and strategy.

- I have sufficient freedom and authority to do my job well.

- My role aligns with my personal purpose and values.

Again, based on personal preferences, some attributes may be more important to an employee than others.

ENVIRONMENT

The next bucket is about the work environment. This is about how it feels to be a part of your team. Several factors make up a good working environment: open two-way communication; involvement in key issues; collaboration; respect; a sense of community; fairness; and a culture of high performance. In the next few paragraphs, I lay out some simple ideas about how to create a work environment in which people can flourish.

COMMUNICATION

The first thing people expect from their manager is that the manager gives them adequate time and understands their needs. This involves creating an environment in which open and honest two-way communication takes place. Unless managers regularly reach out and talk to their employees, and similarly encourage employees to approach them when needed, it is impossible to get a sense of what is important to employees. Without this knowledge, they cannot align personal aspirations with organizational goals, and therefore cannot release untapped energy. The normal reaction from managers when they hear this is that they don't have enough time in their day to give each team member as much attention as they need. On the contrary, those who understand this simple idea know that they don't have enough time in the day because of the fact that they are not investing enough time in their people.

Most managers end up firefighting or doing the work themselves because they are disappointed by their subordinates' output. If they have created an environment of open communication and ask the question, Why is this subordinate output a problem?, chances are they will realize it is less about the subordinates' abilities and more about mismatched expectations caused by poor communication. Let's get one thing straight: Most employees like to succeed, and don't want to disappoint their superiors. They expect their managers to invest enough time in them so that they fully understand what it takes to succeed. Great managers understand that to save time, you have to invest time in your subordinates.

INVOLVEMENT AND GUIDED DISCOVERY

Most people like to be involved in key issues and want their opinions to be considered before key decisions are made. As their manager, do you actively seek and value their input? My manager during my Goldman Sachs days, Steve Kerr, is one of the world's foremost leadership and management experts. Do a search and read anything written by him and you will immediately know what a great thinker he is. Yet even with his stature and expertise, I never once heard him give us (his subordinates) a command. While he almost always knew exactly how we should proceed on a project, rather than telling us, he would ask our "expert" opinion. If our suggestions were not in sync with what he knew to be right, he would gently nudge us toward the right place by asking guiding questions. In the end, we did exactly what he wanted us to, but walked away feeling like doing so was our idea. This is a simple technique—I call it "guided discovery"—whereby instead of giving someone the answer, you ask questions in a way that leads the individual toward the answer so that they feel it is *their* solution. Try it, it is not too difficult.

COLLABORATION

With the exception of a few people who prefer to work alone, the average employee in a large organization likes and expects to work in a collaborative culture. With increasing business complexity, collaboration across internal silos is a must. Excessive internal competition becomes a source of stress for most people, and diminishes the organization's ability to win in the marketplace. I often ask my seminar participants: How many people have been in at least one situation when internal competition or the lack of collaboration led to a delay on a project or some other kind of inferior result? I sometimes follow up with: What was the cost of such a situation? You can imagine the answers—every single participant raises their hand.

In one instance, while everyone raised their hand, they started laughing. When I asked what was funny, one of them asked me, "What do you mean by 'at least one situation,' we experience this every day." The point is simple. As a manager, your job is to maximize positive emotional energy. Unhealthy internal competition drains energy and takes an organization away from its core mission. If you are not proactive about creating an environment of trust and collaboration, human potential will be wasted. The cost of inaction is huge.

RESPECT AND DIGNITY

At the end of the day, all of us want to be treated with respect and dignity at work. Before you dismiss this as obvious, consider this: Most managers are unaware when they treat their people in a disrespectful way. In the multicultural and interconnected world we live in today, we work with people from many different backgrounds. If managers don't take the trouble of understanding different cultural values and norms, it is easy to disrespect people without intending to.

I once coached a manager in New York who had several Asians (from Japan and China) on his team. While he was largely considered a good manager, his 360 feedback reports always showed low scores on treating people with respect. The numbers revealed that only a certain section of his team rated him low on this dimension. Upon investigation, it turned out that his Asian subordinates were the ones who felt disrespected. I asked them if the manager was rude or abusive in any way, and they said no. On the contrary, he was one of the politest people they've known, they told me. Did he not understand their culture and was he offending them with his insensitivity toward Asian values? Again they said no, and told me how great a job he did in trying to understand and respect Asian values. Then how did he treat them disrespectfully? I asked. It turned out that when there were important issues facing the business that the manager needed to consult others about, he always talked to people on the team who were most similar to him, and those were the colleagues who were bred and educated in America. When it came to discussing difficult issues over a beer after work, he never consulted the Asians. It was always the American business school "buddies." Even though the manager was fair in every other way, and did not intend to disrespect anyone, the Asians felt insulted about being left out of the inner circle.

When I discussed this with the manager, he was surprised. He told me that the only reason he did not talk to the Asians about this was that the usual topic of discussion was how to handle his superiors, who were all American. He thought only his fellow Americans, or those on the team who had grown up in the United States, would be able to understand the problems and would therefore be able to give guidance on the situation. He clearly had no intention of offending anyone.

Giving negative or corrective feedback in public is another easy way of disrespecting someone. Corrective feedback must always be given privately.

COMMUNITY AND FRIENDSHIP

Given the ever-increasing number of work hours, employees expect an environment of community and friendship. As lives are getting busier, the number of people who don't know their neighbors is increasing worldwide. For many, the only avenue to satisfy the human need of belonging to a community is the workplace. Studies have shown that employees who have good friends at work tend to be more energized than those who do not.

FAIRNESS

Another common expectation is that of fairness. Most people like to work with full integrity and diligence, and generally try to perform to the best of their abilities. In return they expect to be evaluated and rewarded fairly. The fairness of compensation and reward is often more important than their size. The amount of money people make is important, but fairness is even more important.

HIGH-PERFORMANCE CULTURE

Finally, achievement-oriented employees like an environment that demands high performance and where mediocrity is not tolerated. Nothing de-motivates a hardworking employee more than widespread tolerance for nonperformance. Achievement-oriented people like to be challenged, and like to work with other achievement-oriented people. Who do you like to play your favorite sport with—someone slightly better than you or someone worse than you? In which of the two cases does the standard of your own game fall below your normal level?

Summing up, for an employee to be highly engaged and energized at work, he/she must strongly agree with the following seven statements regarding his/her work environment:

- My manager regularly engages with me and has a good sense of what is important to me.

- My opinion on important issues is sought and valued.

- Our organization has a culture in which people collaborate rather than compete with one another.

- Everyone in our organization is treated with respect and dignity.

- Our organization has an environment of community and friendship.

- Our organization has a fair reward and recognition system in place.

- Our organization has a culture of high performance where mediocrity is not accepted.

DEVELOPMENT

The third bucket is development. This set of expectations deals with most employees' need for growth. With the ever-increasing rate of change in business, lifetime employment has become a thing of the past. New technologies are making traditional businesses obsolete at an alarming rate, and as a result the average person is changing jobs more often than before. Hardly anyone expects lifetime employment anymore, but they do expect lifetime employability. While choosing between jobs, candidates often opt for the one that offers better prospects in terms of learning and development. Managers who have a reputation for investing the time in developing their people tend to have an easier time attracting the best talent. If you pause here for a moment and think about the best managers you have ever worked for, you will probably pick someone you learned a lot from.

OPPORTUNITIES TO LEARN AND GROW

In order to continually develop their skills, high-achieving people like to be staffed on challenging assignments. They do not shy away from high-profile work and are willing to take risks. They also like to receive regular feedback and coaching on their performance, and seek out managers who are willing to do so.

DEVELOPING STRENGTHS FURTHER

For them to be highly energized, employees want their managers to help identify and develop their strengths further. Contrary to conventional wisdom, most people have more room for improvement in an area of natural talent rather than an area of weakness. This is hard to understand at first, but think about this: If you have a shot at being great at something, which is it more likely to be—something that you are already good at, or something that you have not yet had much success in? Talent is not a mathematical equation. To go from good to great, you have to possess some natural talent. Most managers do not understand this, and continue to focus their development investment and feedback on their subordinates' weaknesses. Despite the best of intentions on the part of managers, most performance review discussions tend to deflate employees instead of energizing them. This is largely because the bulk of the discussion focuses on one or two things that the employee does not do well. A typical one-hour performance review discussion goes something like this:

> **Manager:** You've done a great job at x, y, z, a, b, and c. We really value your contribution here. Thank you, and keep up the good work. *(5 minutes)*

> **Employee:** Thank you, I enjoy my work and try to do my best. *(Employee begins to feel good, and expects the manager to talk in a bit more detail about all the things that have gone well.)*

> **Manager:** Now let us focus on the areas that need improvement. There are a couple of things you could do a lot better at, and I want to spend the rest of our time discussing those. I think as

you progress in your career, these things are going to become increasingly important, so we should address them . . . *(55 minutes) (Employee is immediately deflated and feels undervalued for all the things that went well.)*

There is no mention about picking a strength or two and talking about how to develop it further so that the individual can go from good to great.

When it comes to the development of our children, what do most parents do when they see their child showing natural talent at music, a sport, or a particular academic stream? They focus on it and help their child develop it further, they organize private lessons, and go to great lengths to give the child every opportunity to excel at the things he or she seems to have some natural talent in. Most parents prioritize the talent areas over other areas because they fully understand that the return on investment will be greater if they focus on natural talent areas. In fact, if a parent keeps pushing a child in an area where the child does not have natural talent, over time the child loses confidence and her performance drops even in areas in which she is strong. Yet, as managers, at work we often tend to do the reverse. We focus almost exclusively on weaknesses. This is a lose-lose strategy because contrary to conventional wisdom, both the employee and the organization tend to gain more if the focus is on developing strengths rather than overcoming weaknesses.

According to Marcus Buckingham and Curt Coffman, the best managers help their subordinates in understanding a bit more about who they really are, and in putting their strengths to work. I was a currency trader in the early years of my career, but regularly spoke at conferences and seminars when opportunities arose. At the request of HR, I also gave training sessions to fellow employees from time to time. I was a good trader, and enjoyed my job. I also enjoyed the prestige that came with it. However, the best advice I ever got in my early career was from Raghu Krishnamoorthy, then head of HR for American Express

Bank in India, and now a senior HR officer at General Electric. Watching me perform at the seminars and training sessions, he noticed I had a natural talent and passion for teaching and public speaking. When the head-of-training position on his team became vacant, he called me to his office to discuss my interest in it. I was flattered to be offered the job but quickly refused. I liked my job—it was cool to be a trader—why would I ever think about moving to HR of all places? Raghu asked me to curb my trader instinct of quick decision making and think about it over the weekend, and to honestly evaluate my natural strengths and passion before deciding one way or the other. "Sleep over it, and dig deep into your heart before deciding," he said.

His point was straightforward: If you work in an area of natural strength and passion, you will be extremely successful and have a lot of fun at the same time. To cut a long story short, I did exactly as he suggested, and before the weekend was over, I was convinced that it was the right move for me. My family and friends could not understand why I wanted to give up a lucrative career as a trader and move into Human Resources, so it was one of the loneliest decisions of my life, but by far the best. I made the move over sixteen years ago, and have never stopped having fun.

The biggest gift a manager can give subordinates is to help them build on their strengths. Raghu did exactly that for me, but most managers miss this huge opportunity. Even while there was no real need here, Raghu saw something and helped me build what would turn out to be an amazingly satisfying career. This is what great managers are made of. Having benefited from Raghu's leadership, I have tried to do the same for as many people as possible over the years since. Some of my best (and most gratifying) moments as a leader have happened when I have been able to help someone find their strengths, passion, and focus.

You are probably thinking: "But what about critical weaknesses?" What if an employee needs to perform certain tasks really well in order to succeed on the job? Here's a simple rule of thumb: If the employee needs to perform ten tasks really well in order to excel at a job, and if six to eight of them are areas of weakness, then the employee should be removed from that particular job. That is a clear sign of a poor job fit. If, on the other hand, the employee is good at seven to eight out of the ten tasks and is weak on one or two, you need to ask yourself how critical those two tasks are to overall success. If they are very critical, then you need to help the employee get to a level where they can perform to an acceptable level, but accept that this might never be an area of strength. If the tasks are not particularly critical to success, then you should not worry about it, and focus your development efforts on an area of strength. Nobody can be good at everything. It is impossible. The art of managing and leading people is all about getting the best out of people by leveraging and growing their strengths and neutralizing critical weaknesses.

On average, if you invest one hundred units of time and money on someone's development, I would recommend at least seventy to eighty of them be invested in developing strengths further. That said, you need to act quickly when it becomes clear that a person is in the wrong job. Years ago when I worked for a commercial bank, we promoted a senior currency trader to be the head of the trading room. He had a proven track record of successful trading over a number of years. Initially he was elated with the promotion. However, soon after, his individual performance as a trader began to fall. The team's overall performance began to suffer, too. People also started complaining about his poor management style and his lack of communication skills. The trader's boss called me to discuss the situation. "As an expert on motivation, what is your advice?" he asked me half jokingly. We discussed the situation and concluded that we had made a mistake in naming the trader as a manager. When we talked to the trader, he told us that he loved to trade, and wanted to do just that. He explained that managing others was not his cup of tea. All he wanted to do was be more successful than anyone else as a trader, and over time wanted to learn how to trade more complex instruments. He also told us of his aspiration to become a proprietary trader one day and move to a bigger financial center like London or New York. We ultimately moved him back to being an individual trader and eventually sent him to New York for a stint on the derivatives desk. He went on from there to become one of the most successful currency derivatives traders for the bank. He was a classic case of a misfit in a managerial role. No amount of managerial training would have helped. As soon as we realized this, we took corrective action and started investing in his strengths again. This helped both the individual and the organization.

ENTREPRENEURSHIP AND INNOVATION

Another way to develop someone is to encourage them to be innovative and entrepreneurial. The best leaders are willing to take some risks and constantly urge their employees to think out of the box to come up with innovative ideas to increase commercial impact. Most corporate settings tend to dismiss creative ideas before they even have a chance to be fully evaluated. If you really want to continue winning in the marketplace and develop your people at the same time, consider requiring all your people to spend 15 to 20 percent of their time developing new ideas or working on something other than their day job.

CONSTANTLY UPGRADING CAPABILITY

One of the most common traps managers fall into is what I call the "routine of problem solving." Thanks to the ever-increasing pace of business, managers get so busy responding to situations in the normal course of business that they stop thinking. They fail to step back from time to time and ask themselves questions like:

- How is my group performing and what can we do to get better?

- How is the market changing around us and what capabilities will we need to succeed in the future?

- How can we build those capabilities now while we are still fully focused on current opportunities?

As a rule of thumb, at least 5 percent of your total resources should be dedicated to getting ready for the "business of tomorrow."

———————————

For employees to be highly energized, employees must strongly agree with the following six statements about development:

- I am given challenging assignments that provide me with opportunities to learn and develop.

- I receive regular coaching and feedback on my performance.

- My manager helps me identify my strengths and develop them further.

- Our culture strongly emphasizes entrepreneurship and innovation.

- Our organization constantly strives to upgrade its overall capability to deliver outstanding results.

- I am expected to come up with new ideas to improve efficiency and/or profitability.

RED: HOW TO USE

Many managers I have coached have found the RED framework useful in addressing employee needs and in making their own leadership style more effective. The knowledge of what people want is all-powerful. If you make it your business to find out, you will. With that knowledge, you can align personal aspirations with organizational goals, thereby releasing tremendous energy. At the end of the day, this is not rocket science. It is less about technique and skill and more about how much you sincerely care about energizing others.

The ideas behind RED are applicable to all employees, regardless of their level. Everyone thinks about his/her role, environment, and development, and managers at all levels can use these ideas. The only thing that changes, depending upon the seniority of your subordinates, is the sophistication of your conversations with them, and perhaps the magnitude of the job at hand. Here are some ways to use the RED framework:

PULSE CHECK

The first is to use the nineteen statements to do a periodic survey within your team. Once you get the data back, you can sit down with your team and discuss what you need to do to address issues. You can also use it in your broader organization to get a sense of overall morale. If you choose to do so, there are two options. One: Get your direct reports together and talk about what you need to do about the results. Two: Form a team of people below your directs and ask them to come up with recommendations. You can also do both. If you set up a team of junior people to make recommendations, it is a good idea to have someone from your direct reports team act as a sponsor. The survey instrument could look like the one shown on page 69.

Please state your level of agreement or disagreement with the following statements using a 1 – 5 scale: 1 = Strongly Disagree, 2 = Disagree, 3 = Neutral, 4 = Agree, 5 = Strongly Agree					
#	ITEM	1	2	3	4	5
1	Our organization has a compelling vision for its future success					
2	We have an effective/differentiated strategy to achieve the vision					
3	I have challenging (stretch) but achievable goals					
4	I clearly understand how my work fits into the overall vision and strategy					
5	I have sufficient freedom and authority to do my job well					
6	My role aligns with my personal purpose and values					
7	My manager regularly engages with me and has a good sense of what is important to me					
8	My opinion on important issues is sought and valued					
9	Our organization has a culture in which people collaborate rather than compete with one another					
10	Everyone in our organization is treated with respect and dignity					
11	Our organization has an environment of community and friendship					
12	Our organization has a fair reward and recognition system in place					
13	Our organization has a culture of high performance where mediocrity is not accepted					
14	I am given challenging assignments that provide me with opportunities to learn and develop					
15	I receive regular coaching and feedback on my performance					
16	My manager helps me identify my strengths and develop them further					
17	Our culture strongly emphasizes entrepreneurship and innovation					
18	Our organization constantly strives to upgrade its overall capability to deliver outstanding results					
19	I am expected to come up with new ideas to improve efficiency and/or profitability					
	ANY OTHER COMMENTS/SUGGESTIONS:					

This instrument is based on my practical experience as a leader and as a consultant. I have used it with my clients all over the world, and it returns very meaningful information for leaders who want to significantly increase employee engagement.

TARGETED CONVERSATIONS

Another good way is to use this set of questions as a framework for individual discussions. Whenever you have a moment with a subordinate, ask a question related to some aspect of RED. The more you ask, the more information you will get about your staff's preferences. Armed with this information, you will be able to address their concerns during the day-to-day course of business. You don't even have to use the term "RED." Make it your own language. Whenever I am with a subordinate, either in a one-on-one update meeting or even riding in a cab to see a client, I ask questions like:

> ➤ So how do you think we are doing overall? Do you think we are focused on the right things in order to have maximum impact? *(Role)*

> ➤ How are you feeling? How are others feeling? Are people having fun? *(Environment)*

> ➤ I know you're busy, but what are you doing to invest in yourself? Where do you see yourself in five or ten years? What are you doing to build toward that destination? *(Development)*

Such conversations can be short—around the watercooler, as they say. The important thing is to keep the dialogue going. RED just gives you a mental framework to narrow it down to a few manageable things. This can be a particularly useful tool while communicating with people two levels below you. Asking junior people some questions along the lines of RED will give you great information about the managers who work directly below you. You can use the information to coach them better. I often ask people a couple of levels below me in my company to describe to me the overall strategy of their department. I follow that up with a question about their own role. If I don't hear crisp and confident responses, I know that the manager of that team has work to do in terms of clarifying roles and responsibilities.

LABEL AND LINK

When assigning work, speak to the individual about why it might be good for them. If it will help them succeed at their goals (Role), tell them. If it will stretch them and give them new experiences (Development), tell them. If it aligns with their personal purpose and values, remind them. The most flawed assumption about communication is this: People have the ability to know what is good for them and will recognize growth opportunities when they see them. The reality is quite the contrary. If you expect people to guess and put two and two together, the truth is, they often don't. I am not suggesting that people are generally not smart enough. I am saying that what is obvious to you might not be to them, so labeling it, linking it, and spelling it out is not a bad thing. Don't leave it to chance if another minute of conversation can make sure you are on the same page.

MAKE IT A COMMON LANGUAGE

Insist that your direct reports use the RED framework with their teams. While it is not necessary to use the RED terminology, it helps to have a common language. If everyone understands RED and its components, your team can save time by getting straight to the issue. In a team meeting, if you are discussing lack of performance, you can label the issue by asking: Is this a role, environment, or development issue?

WHAT DOESN'T WORK

Unfortunately, instead of trying to really understand employees' needs, many managers use stock techniques to motivate their people, and end up implementing initiatives that are well intended but ill conceived. Here's what doesn't work:

- *Putting them in your shoes.* Most managers think about what motivates them, and assume that the same things will motivate everyone else. A manager who cares most about money and not much else is likely to make the mistake of assuming the same might be true for his/her subordinates. I have known many people who believe that as long as they are paid extremely well, they don't really care about any other factors related to the workplace. As mature adults, they believe, people ought to be able to take care of themselves, and not complain about anything as long as they are getting paid. They fail to make an effort to understand how each of their subordinates is motivated and, as a result, also fail to drive the highest possible performance. In fact, the superior monetary rewards they dole out might actually be wasted. A few simple conversations, and a regular dialogue, can prevent this.

  Similarly, a manager who values freedom and autonomy above all else might assume the same is true for others. "I like what I do and am good at it. I don't need my manager breathing down my neck, and like the fact that he leaves me alone," said one manager whom I was coaching. His 360 feedback report said that he did not spend enough time with his subordinates. When I probed to find out what was going on, I found out pretty quickly that he had assumed that how he liked to work with his manager was the right thing for everyone.

- *One-size-fits-all initiatives.* Across-the-board initiatives (such as casual Fridays or afternoon fruits) do not motivate everyone equally. Each of us is motivated differently. Clearly, there is a place for large, organization-wide initiatives and people policies. I don't have a problem with those. All I am trying to emphasize is that those broad initiatives and people-friendly policies are not a substitute for individual relationships and conversations.

- *Pep talks and motivational speeches.* Leaders with charisma and a gift for public speaking tend to overrely on this strength. At the end of the day, each individual is motivated by some kind of self-interest alone, and the effects of motivational speeches are short-lived at best. Leaders that talk the talk without dramatic results make it even worse. Over time their lack of sincerity, or the difference between their words and actions, causes a drop in motivation among the troops.

- *Team-building activities.* A lot of time and money is invested in so-called team-building activities. How many times have you been asked to go on a team-building trip or seminar where you were made to participate in exercises such as letting yourself fall backward knowing your colleagues will support you before you hit the floor? You are supposed to come back from such "outward bound" trips more energized. While they sometimes give a temporary boost to interpersonal relationships within a team, any change is short-lived. Trust-based relationships can only be formed over time and through consistent caring behavior.

- *Money.* As stated earlier, paying people tons of money certainly keeps them coming back to work. Without a certain threshold of compensation, you cannot attract or retain top talent. However, money releases only rational energy, and does not have the power of releasing emotional energy.

When I asked an entrepreneur friend of mine why he decided to quit a very senior position at a large organization to start out on his own, he replied without hesitation, "I got tired of working for stupid people." Another executive who was in between jobs said to me, "If I can help it, I never want to work inside a large corporation ever again." I asked him to explain why he felt so strongly, and he said, "Most of the bosses I've worked for seem to be obsessed with just one thing—satisfying their own ego. Not only did they seldom bother to find out what I wanted or needed, they placed their own ego needs even above the needs of the business." While there is nothing wrong with self-interest, as a leader you have to get into the habit of focusing on your employees' needs. In the increasingly complex business landscape of today, ensuring that your employees are fully energized is not optional. It is vital.

No one understood this idea better than Jack Ma, the founder of the Alibaba Group in China. His flagship company, Alibaba.com, is today the global leader in business-to-business e-commerce. Founded in 1999, Alibaba.com makes it easy for millions of buyers and suppliers around the world to do business online through three marketplaces: a global trade marketplace (www.alibaba.com) for importers and exporters, a Chinese marketplace (www.alibaba.com.cn) for domestic trade in China, and, through an associated company, a Japanese marketplace (www.alibaba.co.jp) facilitating trade to and from Japan. Together, its marketplaces form a community of more than 45 million registered users. Jack Ma grew up in Hangzhou, China. Throughout his student years he struggled with math, and he failed his college admission test twice before finally earning acceptance. After teaching English to himself, he began to offer free tour-guide services to Western tourists so that he could practice speaking the language, eventually becoming an English teacher.

It was on his first trip to the United States in 1995 that he learned about the Internet. Immediately realizing its potential, he started China's first Internet company in the same year, even though he had no background in computer science or technology. After struggling to make it profitable for over two years, he eventually sold the company and spent the next fourteen frustrating months building Web pages for the Ministry of Foreign Trade in Beijing. After unsuccessfully dabbling with Internet-related businesses for four years, he gathered his original team of eighteen together and announced his decision to return to Hangzhou to start a new company. According to Liu Shiying and Martha Avery in their book *Alibaba*, here is what Jack said to his team at this meeting:

> I am giving you three choices. First, you can go and work with Yahoo! I will recommend you and I know that the company will not only welcome you but the salaries will be high. Second, you can go to work for Sina or Sohu: they'll similarly welcome you and the salaries won't be too bad. Or third, you can come home with me. However, you'll get just $95 in salary per month, rent your own flat, and live within a five-minute radius of where I live, because in order to save money I won't allow you to take taxis, and moreover you'll have to work in my home. You make your own decision.

Even though he allowed them three days to make a decision, they told him within three minutes that every single one of them was ready to go back home with him.

Among Ma's key strengths was his remarkable ability to align the hopes and aspirations of his team members with the overall mission. Alibaba has generally paid lower salaries compared to the rest of the market. Yet they have never had any trouble attracting and retaining the best talent. They understand that the key to motivated staff is not trying to motivate them, but understanding their preexisting motivation triggers and aligning them to the overall mission.

RED is not a catchy formula or another management fad. It is what most people care about, and my attempt here was to package it for you in a way that is easy to understand and practical to use. Ultimately, success will depend on how much personal energy you devote to energizing others. It will be your seriousness of purpose, and not a technique like RED, that will determine how effective you are. Use whatever works for you—RED, blue, green, or any other color, but do it sincerely. If managing others' energy seems tedious to you, strongly consider a line of work that does not involve doing so. If you want to remain in the energy-management business, hopefully the above information will be of some use to you.

PART TWO

Enterprise Leadership

3

GALVANIZE Large Numbers: Enterprise Leadership

In this and the next three chapters, I will talk interchangeably about enterprise and organizational leadership. Let me first clearly define what I mean by enterprise or organizational leadership. Regardless of size and scope, you become an enterprise or organizational leader when the number of people under your command is so large that it is not possible for you to have a close one-to-one relationship with everyone, and when there are more than two levels of organizational hierarchy below you. In other words, if your direct reports have teams under them, and if the total number of people in your organization is greater than your ability to manage everyone personally, you are an enterprise leader. You could be the CEO of a company with hundreds of thousands of employees, or a functional leader within a company with only a hundred people under you. As long as the two conditions above are true, the contents of the next four chapters should be extremely useful to you.

Energizing a whole organization, or large numbers of people, is different from energizing yourself or your direct reports individually. When you try to galvanize the energy of large numbers of people, you first need to make a transition from being a self and/or team leader to an enterprise leader. For many, this is the hardest career transition because the rules for success at the enterprise level are different from the time-tested rules that earned them all their success and promotions until this time in their careers. The very actions and qualities that make a person successful until they embark upon an enterprise leadership position might actually become the reason for failure from this point onward.

Typically, a successful executive invited to an enterprise leadership position gets there by following the familiar path of individual achievement. Chances are, she was a straight-A student throughout school, worked incredibly hard through school with the sole objective of getting into a top-notch college, and did well at college, displaying both academic and extracurricular excellence. She knew the rules of success that her parents instilled in her—hard work, perseverance, personal drive, and focus. At the end of the day, success depended upon how hard she was able to drive herself and how consistently she was able to push herself to the limit in order to get the best possible results. She probably grew up hearing advice like, "If you are willing to work hard, anything is possible" or "It is up to you, what you get out of it depends on what you put into it." Reaping the benefits of this work ethic, she probably landed a coveted job of her choice, and had a very successful run for the first few years as an individual contributor, because the rules of success were still the same. Then she became a team leader. At this point, besides driving her own self, she had to care for her team. She probably continued her success because though she was the manager of a team, a lot of the team's success depended on her own contributions. If someone on the team was not able to perform as needed, she would just do it herself. Because she was so strong individually, any weakness in leading and managing people was probably overlooked.

But now she has been invited to be an enterprise leader. She needs to lead a whole organization to success. This is where she gets into trouble, because now it is not about her alone. In fact, it is not about her at all. Now she needs to facilitate the success of others. Rather than producing results herself, she needs to create conditions that enable large numbers of people to create the desired results. Often, she doesn't even get credit for the success of the organization, and she needs to be fine with that. She needs to put self-interest on the back burner in the interest of the organization as a whole. The very technical skills that got her promoted up to this point now become less important, and the one thing she did not pay enough attention to—leading people— becomes her full-time job. Going back to the beginning of this book, what she needs to be clear about is whether she really wants to lead or to continue as an individual producer. If she has not thought through her purpose and values carefully, she is now in trouble. She could be in a position similar to the accidental parent who did not want to have children. Even if leading an organization is what she wants, she still has to make the most critical transition of all—*from "I" to "we."*

Approximately three in every four careers derail at the point of this critical transition. It is ironic that so many people work so hard to attain a leadership position all their adult lives only to be derailed when they get the coveted prize. So the first step toward successful enterprise leadership is to be totally clear that you want it and to fully understand what is involved. Go back to the first chapter to refresh your memory: This is not a glamorous job; take it only if you fully understand what is involved. Even though you are the big boss now, even though you are more powerful than ever before, the factors of success are not as much in your control as they used to be.

What is common among Richard Thoman at Xerox, Durk Jager at Procter & Gamble, Richard McGinn at Lucent Technologies, Doug Ivestor at Coca-Cola, and Jill Bared at Mattel Inc.? According to Jay Conger and David Nadler, they are all examples of leaders at high-profile companies who flamed out early in their tenures. Were they unable to successfully make the transition from "I" to "we"? Conger and Nadler describe the problem beautifully in their 2004 *MIT Sloan Management Review* article titled "When CEOs Step Up to Fail." According to them, *most CEOs are biased toward either "content"—the substance of a com-*

pany's business—or "context"—the environment in which decisions are made. In today's complex organizations, executives who lack strong context skills may have difficulty navigating the transition to power. Conger and Nadler further explain content orientation as focusing on the substance of the business, and content-oriented leaders as those interested and capable in the core strategy, technology, or financial structure of the business. In other words, these are functional leaders who understand some technical or strategic aspects of a business very well. Context-oriented leaders, on the other hand, are more interested in the overall environment in which business is done, and are focused on values, purpose, the interactions of the executive team, and on facilitating enterprise success as a whole. Jim Collins, author of the international bestseller *Good to Great,* describes the requirements of enterprise leadership in a similar way. According to him, if you want to be a successful "level 5" leader—someone who builds sustainable organizational success over the long term—you need to be more ambitious about creating a durable organization and less ambitious about orchestrating your own personal success, fame, and fortune. So, as I've said before, the first step is to make sure you are ready for enterprise leadership in terms of your personal orientation.

Once you've decided that leadership is what you really want, the question becomes: How can you be most effective? The rest of this chapter and the next three chapters focus on this key question. I will try to identify for you the most important levers you need to pull as an enterprise leader, and give you a simple but powerful system with which to manage and grow your business. As complexity continues to increase, no one individual can control all aspects of a business. This has become even truer with the evolution of technology, where business boundaries are becoming less relevant and work is distributed around the globe. What should the leader focus his or her *own* energy on? What are the most important aspects of the business? For a team leader these answers were reasonably straightforward: You listed everything that needed to be done and assigned specific responsibilities to each team member, while keeping the most complex or important tasks (like managing the most important client relationships) to yourself. You probably were able to check every team member's work, and were able to bring it all together to get the results you wanted. You were still in control. Now you run a large business or function, and you cannot possibly manage it all yourself. You have to delegate control. So what should you focus on personally? If you don't think about this question very carefully before sitting in the big chair, you will set yourself up for failure.

Before you know it, all kinds of things will start appearing on your desk. The production folks will want help with product improvement, while sales and marketing will want to get you involved with an important client. At the same time, the legal department will want your attention on an important regulatory issue, and Human Resources will want you to approve a new compensation plan. How will you prioritize? Before long, you will be overwhelmed. Thanks to technology, you are already overloaded with information. The rate at which e-mails, phone calls, and other modes of communication are reaching you, you are already working 24/7.

All these successful careers that derail upon reaching an enterprise leadership position do not derail for want of hard work. If anything, during the period just before derailment, those people probably worked harder than ever. But at this stage it is not about how hard or how long you work, it is about what you work on and what you delegate. What should you do to maximize your contribution to the overall success of your business?

BRAINS—BONES—NERVES

Your full-time job now should be to create conditions in which your people can do their work successfully. You need to put in place a few important frameworks within which a large number of people can operate in a way that maximizes their energy. How can you do that? By controlling and shaping the three most important levers of sustainable business growth—the *brains,* the *bones,* and the *nerves.*

- The *brains* of a business is its vision and strategy, and here the enterprise leader must shape and set direction.

- The *bones* are the organizational architecture, and here the enterprise leader must design the organization in order to execute the strategy.

- The *nerves* refer to the culture and climate of the organization, and here the enterprise leader must foster a culture of long-lasting excellence.

Just as the human body needs all three systems—the brain, bones, and nerves—functioning in perfect harmony to maximize longevity and performance, a business needs its strategy, architecture, and culture to work in harmony in order to maximize results. As an enterprise leader, you should focus on these three as your most important focus areas; everything else must be delegated.

As I describe the three pillars of sustainable growth to executives in my seminars and training programs, every now and then someone raises their hand and asks, "So what's so new about focusing on vision and strategy, organization design, and culture? As senior leaders, don't we already know that this is where we need to start?" Agreed, there is nothing new about focusing on the three pillars. However, the key is in *staying focused* on them. A common mistake bosses make is to think that setting direction, designing the organization, and defining the culture are only periodic activities. They assume that setting direction (vision and strategy) is something you do once every year or once every few years. They believe organizational design is also an activity that happens only at the start of a business or at the time of a major shift in business conditions. Similarly, they think once cultural values have been defined, they are done with the "soft" issue of culture.

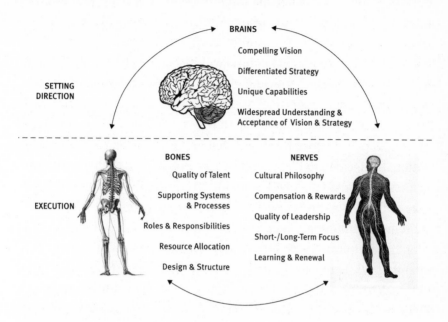

Brains–Bones–Nerves

Nothing could be further from the truth. A major difference between bosses and leaders is that unlike bosses, leaders know that to drive long-term growth, they need to manage the brains, bones, and nerves of their business all year long, every year. They understand that this is their full-time job. It is not just where you start as leaders, it is where you *stay* as leaders.

ALIBABA.COM: OPENING UP A WHOLE NEW UNIVERSE

According to Martha Avery and Liu Shiying, authors of *Alibaba,* Jack Ma of Alibaba.com was able to make the transition into enterprise leadership successfully, but not without making almost disastrous mistakes. By the time Ma and his team started work on founding Alibaba .com, they had already been at the forefront of the Internet revolution in China. Through his work at the Ministry of Foreign Trade, Ma had become familiar with the government's macroeconomic policies. It was abundantly clear that in 1999 China was just at the beginning of a huge wave of e-commerce that would change the way the world does business forever. The possibilities were endless, but his experience with China Yellow Pages had taught Ma that to succeed in the Internet space, one had to be very specific about what to pursue. After careful consideration, he decided to focus on business-to-business (B2B) rather than business-to-consumer (B2C) e-commerce. He realized that the backbone of China's export-oriented economy was made up of millions of small and medium-size enterprises (SMEs). However, without an efficient "marketplace," both buyers and sellers were suboptimizing their potential. While buyers around the world found it difficult to identify and reach Chinese suppliers, sellers (largely SMEs) were being squeezed out by big buyers like Walmart and/or by intermediaries. What if there was a "place" where buyers and sellers could meet directly and transact business? What if the small guys could look all over the world for customers, and compete for business without huge marketing and business development costs? It was with these questions in mind that Ma and his team of eighteen founders set the vision and mission and goals of Alibaba.com (as described by Avery and Shiying).

MISSION:

To make it easy to do business anywhere

GOALS:

1. Set up a company that lasts for 102 years

2. Establish a company that focuses on providing services to China's SMEs

3. Create the world's largest e-commerce company

Ma and his founding team did an excellent job of defining the *brains* of their business. The strategy was straightforward. Alibaba .com would become a marketplace for importers and exporters where exporters would be able to set up storefronts to showcase their products and services. Buyers would be able to browse this information for free, but sellers would pay a fee for listing their products and services. Over time, Alibaba would also provide additional value-added services such as providing reference and quality checks, and facilitating a safe and cost-effective payment system between buyers and sellers. And similar to a lot of leaders we studied (like Howard Schultz, Jeff Bezos, and Tom Gardner), they took a long-term view about their company and business. Notice their desire to set up a company that lasts 102 years.

Success came early to Alibaba, which had been started with initial capital of only $60,000 provided by eighteen founders. Within a year, Alibaba received two infusions of capital totaling $25 million from Goldman Sachs and SoftBank. With abundance of cash at the time of the now famous dot-com crash of 2000–2001, Ma decided to go big, and began a wild expansion that nearly brought the company to the brink of disaster. Over the course of a very short period of time, Alibaba had expanded operations into London, Hong Kong, Korea, and Silicon Valley in California. Within one year, Alibaba had become a multinational company with employees from thirteen countries. The company had already lost money ever since its inception, and Ma realized he was losing control. This is a typical outcome of not paying enough attention to designing the "bones" correctly. Ma found himself in a position where it was impossible to manage the disparate parts of the business based all over the globe. The team in Hong Kong was convinced that reaching the capital markets was the most important thing, while the team of techies in the company's Silicon Valley development center was focused more on cool technology and less on business needs. Others had strong opinions as well, and while they all fought hard to have their voices heard, Ma realized he had a problem which he summarized to authors Liu Shiying and Martha Avery as follows: "The hardest thing in the world is to have fifty hypersmart people sitting in a room trying to get something done." Needless to add, costs were spiraling out of control.

A quick learner, Ma realized his mistake of overzealous expansion and launched a strategic reorientation. He announced a reduction in force at the end of 2000, and hired a seasoned business manager from General Electric as his chief operating officer to design strong bones and help turn the company around. A big part of the problem was the scattered nature of the business. For example, Alibaba's Web site was based in Silicon Valley even while the bulk of its business was in China. Another problem caused by rapid expansion was that many people had strayed away from the core mission of the company and had very different ideas about what success would look like. Some were just staying on to gain financially from the forthcoming IPO. Ma called this strategic reorientation the "return to China." Between 2001 and 2003 he centralized some of the operations back in China, purged the ranks of nonbelievers—people who did not share a sense of common purpose and mission—and instituted rigorous training for salespeople.

Of all the activities in the strategic reorientation, perhaps the most important was refocusing people on the core ideology behind Alibaba. Right from the start, Jack Ma was clear about one thing: His company would focus on providing the maximum possible value to his customers. The primary mission of the company was to help SMEs in growing their business. Making a reasonable profit was the secondary mission. Ten years after starting Alibaba.com, while addressing a gathering at the Asia Society in New York, Ma reflected as follows on the financial crisis of 2008: "The main reason for the crisis is that people stopped focusing on maximizing customer value, and became fixated on shareholder value instead. Stop focusing only on making your boss happy, focus also on making the customer happy."

As Alibaba started to turn around and grow again, Ma and his team realized that in order to stay united and focused on the main mission, the company needed a common set of values which would guide behavior. It was time to codify the company's nerves. He articulated the company's six values that until today continue to guide key processes, values like compensation, promotions, performance evaluations, and recruitment. Training sessions routinely remind employees about the values and core philosophy of the company: *We should first help customers make money, then make money (charge a fee) ourselves.*

ALIBABA'S SIX VALUES

1. **Customer First:** The interests of our community of users and paying members must be our first priority.

2. **Teamwork:** We expect our employees to collaborate as a team. We encourage input from our employees in the decision-making process, and expect every employee to commit to the team's objectives.

3. **Embrace Change:** We operate in a fast-evolving industry. We ask our employees to maintain flexibility, continue to innovate and adapt to new business conditions and practice.

4. **Integrity:** Integrity is at the heart of our business as trust is an essential element of a marketplace. We expect our employees to uphold the highest standards of integrity and to deliver on their commitments.

5. **Passion:** Our employees are encouraged to act with passion whether it is serving customers or developing new services and products.

6. **Commitment:** Our employees have a dedicated focus and commitment to understanding and delivering on the needs of Chinese and global SMEs.

By proactively staying focused on the brains, bones, and nerves of the company, Ma built a strong organization that continued to go from strength to strength over the ten years. The rest, as they say, is history. In the next three chapters I attempt to give you a few simple but powerful ideas about how to make the leap into leading a larger workforce by shaping and managing the brains, bones, and nerves of *your* organization most effectively.

4

B-B-N:
Wiring the "Brains"

I recently had the top management (CEO and his thirteen direct reports) of a Fortune 500 company in a room, and asked them two questions:

1. Do you believe your company has a clear strategy?

2. Do you believe it is well understood by everyone in the company?

All thirteen direct reports immediately turned toward the CEO to see how he would respond. As soon as he said yes to both questions, they all joined him in utter agreement. Despite their agreement with the CEO's response, I had a hunch they were not all on the same page. With the CEO's permission, I asked each of them to write down the vision and strategy of the company on a piece of paper and hand it to me. This particular company prided itself on attracting the smartest people and giving them entrepreneurial freedom to run their part of the business. In response to my request, each of the thirteen senior executives in the room wrote a very different picture of the company's vision and strategy. It became clear that each was thinking about just his/her part of the business, but not of the firm as a whole. I suspected that they were probably not doing a good job of cross-selling—recognizing client needs that could be met by another part of the firm—and likely leaving money on the table. Why? Because no one was able to articulate the power of the entire franchise.

My suspicion was confirmed a few hours later when they started openly addressing their weaknesses. While this was a successful company by any standard, they were not unparalleled in their industry. Further discussions during the day revealed that customers often complained that there was no one person in this company who could bring the products of the whole company to them in a seamless way. Customers found it difficult to navigate within the company, and had to deal separately with different silos in order to have their needs met. They found it far easier to deal with the company's largest competitor, if only because the divisions there seemed much more connected, and there was usually one relationship manager who could bring it all together.

If this firm were to maximize its potential in the market, it needed to make sure the silos operated as one integrated group. Selling the whole firm to clients was an integral part of the firm's strategy, yet even the senior most leaders were not behaving in that way. A CEO's primary function is to ensure that senior management fully understands and agrees with the overall direction of the company—to create a whole that is greater than the sum of its parts. Only when senior management is on the same page can there be clarity in the rest of the organization. Very few CEOs do this effectively, and as a result their organizational performance remains suboptimal.

One CEO who understood the importance of articulating strategy was Harvey Golub at American Express. In the 1980s, Golub and his team developed a simple, powerful, and clear mission statement for the company:

TO BE THE WORLD'S MOST RESPECTED SERVICE BRAND

This was long before I moved to the United States, while I was a junior employee at American Express India. I remember Harvey and other senior executives traveled to all American Express locations around the world to explain what that one-line statement meant. They would speak at length about each word: what it represented and why it was chosen. As they listened, it became clear to the thousands of employees across the globe that the company was serious about providing the best possible service. Service was the key word. We also understood the essence of the brand, and what we each needed to do to continually strengthen it. The words "to be" represented that no matter how good we got, we would never stop trying. I heard Harvey speak about this over twenty years ago and still remember it. I have yet to see a better example of creating clarity around the core mission of the company. It is no surprise that when Amex employees are serving customers around the world, they are given liberty to be quick on their feet and to swiftly make decisions that in most scenarios are pleasing to their customers. This is true for all divisions of American Express.

SETTING DIRECTION: FIFTEEN-MINUTE STRATEGY

For an organization to successfully reach a desired destination, the first step is to decide what route to take. In other words, the organization must clearly articulate its objectives and make choices about how it will go about achieving them. This sounds obvious, but in my years of coaching senior executives, I have found that the smartest people tend to overlook or underperform at this primary work of leadership. I am typically brought in as a consultant when an organization is performing below its true potential. By this time the leaders of the business have tried everything (to their minds) possible to "fire up the business." They've tried getting rid of underperformers and have hired quality talent from the competition. They have implemented all kinds of initiatives to incentivize performance. They arrive to me frustrated with their people, failing to understand why in spite of all their repeated efforts their people don't get it.

After listening patiently to their issues, I normally ask them questions similar to the two I posed to the CEO and his thirteen direct reports above: What is your vision for the business, and what strategy do you have in place through which you plan to achieve the vision? I ask them to explain it to me in fifteen minutes or less. If they want to use visuals, I ask them to show it to me all on one to two pages. It is amazing how many leaders I come across who cannot easily answer those questions clearly and crisply. When asked, many talk at length, but are unable to explain clearly and concisely what they hope to create and how they plan to do so.

Some leaders are able to do a better job than others at answering my questions. If they do, I follow up with another question: Are you confident that all your direct reports can articulate your vision and strategy in the same way as you just did? In many instances, they respond in the negative.

I received my favorite assignment a few years ago when a global head of business asked me for help. He was frustrated because despite the best efforts of his leadership team at repeatedly communicating the business plan, people a few levels below were unable to say what the vision and strategy for the business were. I asked what they had done by way of communication, and he pulled out three spiral-bound documents—each at least two inches thick. He proudly went on to tell me that these were the detailed business plans for each of his three divisions, and that his management team had spent weeks of hard work to put them together. He said, "Our goal was to make sure everyone fully understands what we are trying to accomplish, and no detail was spared. We have nothing to hide." He then went on to tell me how he and his team had traveled to all locations and conducted town hall meetings to explain the strategy, and that these documents had been sent to all employees electronically. "How can anyone in this company claim not to understand our vision and strategy?" he asked in total bewilderment.

I think I offended him when I pointed to the three spiral-bound books and said, "That is your problem." He wanted to know how I could make such a sweeping statement without even looking through the documents, but I insisted that I did not need to. I told him I would look through them later, and that I was sure the strategy was a good one. But the problem was not the lack of thoroughness, it was the length of material. "Find a way to say it simply so that people can understand and accept it," I said. He was not impressed. In fact, he angrily told me that I had no idea how hard he and his team worked on the strategy decks and the great lengths they went to while communicating to the troops. He went on to warn me that if I continued to be so dismissive about clients' work, I would soon be out of business.

When he finally paused for breath, I asked him, "What is more important, the fact that you are right and I am wrong, or the fact that your people still do not understand the strategy?" He paused for a few moments and finally said, "OK, let's get the team together and get to work on simplifying the messages." Over the next few weeks, we worked together to create a one-page picture of the overall strategy, supported by a two-pager on each of the three businesses. We synthesized key messages in such a way that even an outsider like me could understand the power of their mission in fifteen minutes or less.

Before I explain how to communicate a strategy in a powerful way on one page, let me highlight a common issue I come across particularly with very smart executives. I call it the "high-quality, low-acceptance" problem.

SIMPLE, NOT SIMPLISTIC: $Q \times A = E$

My good friend and mentor Steve Kerr has a great way to explain this classic management phenomenon, first articulated by Norman R. F. Maier. Steve maintains that business executives worry too much about the quality of their decisions, and too little about creating widespread acceptance for them. They make the mistake of assuming that if the quality of a decision or strategy is absolutely rock solid, people should have no problem buying into it. After all, nothing is more powerful than science, math, and logic. If the idea makes scientific and/or mathematical sense, and there is data to prove the accuracy and correctness of the idea, why would anyone have a problem? Wrong! Every human has a different brain, and what is obvious to one brain may not be so to another. Steve has a simple but powerful way to explain that leaders need to worry equally, if not more, about creating acceptance. For an idea or strategy to be fully effective, it requires both quality and acceptance. He illustrates this concept with a simple equation:

$$Q \times A = E$$

Q stands for quality. A stands for acceptance, and E is for effectiveness. "The problem with most managers is they don't understand that anything multiplied by zero is zero" he says, and goes on to add, "Another problem we often see is that managers tend to work harder toward improving quality, and don't work enough on improving acceptance." In a large organization, this can make the difference between success and failure.

Here is another simple fact about a multiplication equation: Increasing the smaller of the two variables yields a higher result than increasing the larger variable. Imagine $Q = 7$ and $A = 3$, giving you an overall effectiveness score of 21. According to Steve, most left-brained managers tend to continuously improve quality, and pay little attention to acceptance. So if you increase Q to 8 and keep A at 3, your overall effectiveness increases to 24. Another raise in Q to 9 while keeping the A constant, gives you an effectiveness jump to 27. However, if you do the reverse, i.e., keep Q constant at 7 and increase A to 4, you get an effectiveness of 28. Raise the A to 5 while still keeping Q constant at the original 7 and your effectiveness jumps to 35. At $A = 6$ while Q is still at 7, you get an amazing $E = 42$.

INCREASING Q	INCREASING A
$Q \times A = E$	$Q \times A = E$
7 X 3 = 21	7 X 3 = 21
8 x 3 = 24	7 X 4 = 28
9 X 3 = 27	7 X 5 = 35
10 X 3 = 30	7 x 6 = 42

I often conduct this exercise on a flip chart in front of a roomful of executives. It is absolutely amazing to see the look of disbelief on their faces as they see effectiveness jumping up so rapidly when you increase the A instead of the Q. I joke that you need a degree in advanced variable calculus to understand this deep and complex mathematical concept. The key point is simple: As a leader, you should ask yourself if you have succeeded in creating widespread acceptance. It is harder than most people think.

DEVELOPING BRAINS: CREATING YOUR STRATEGY "STORY"

It should be clear by now that the most efficient and effective "brain" of a business is composed of two elements: one, a compelling vision and strategy articulated with elegant simplicity; two, the ability to achieve acceptance and understanding of the vision and strategy. The next question is how to establish such clarity and acceptance. Again, I want to propose a simple process that allows leaders to tap into the creativity of a large number of people, and enables them to ultimately communicate vision and strategy in a powerful and consistent way.

The task of setting a compelling vision, and establishing a differentiated strategy to achieve the vision, boils down to answering four questions convincingly, consistently, and succinctly. The four questions are: *What, Who, How,* and *Why:*

1. *What* do we want to be?

2. *Who* are our stakeholders?

    a. What do we want to do for each?

3. *How* will we get there?

    a. What is the conventional business model for our industry?

    b. What needs does the conventional model fulfill?

    c. What needs are yet unfulfilled?

    d. What new needs are likely to emerge in the future?

    e. What should we do differently compared to the traditional model?

4. *Why* will we succeed?

    a. What will be our differentiating capabilities?

Once a management team has given enough thought and energy to answering these questions, they must work on articulating the answers in a way that creates clarity, simplicity, and believability, thereby creating widespread acceptance. As stated earlier, packaging the communication is equally important as, if not more important than, the strategy itself.

At its simplest form, a management team should get together and discuss each of these questions, and not give up until they find a convincing set of answers that are energizing. However, given the increasing complexity of business, on one hand, and the ever-increasing need of employees to have greater involvement, on the other, a management team should involve as many people in this strategy-setting process as possible. This can be done by forming multiple teams of people within the organization and asking each team to come up with their version of the answers. Each team should also be asked to package the information in a way that can be articulated powerfully in less than fifteen minutes and/or on no more than one to two pages.

Once each team has had the time to develop their answers (their version of strategy), each team should present their work to a large group composed of all the teams. At the end of all presentations, the best thinking of all groups should be combined to form the final strategy for the business. After the strategy meeting, enough work should be done in drafting a final version to guarantee that it can be articulated clearly in fifteen minutes or less, and cascaded to the entire organization. It is important that all involved in the strategy formulation process as described here should be able to articulate it in a consistent way. It is generally a good idea to convene the group once again to take a final look at the end product and to practice articulating it in a powerful and consistent way. Members of the strategy formulation group should ultimately become spokespeople for the strategy and use every possible opportunity to communicate it repeatedly to the rest of the organization. This may sound like a large investment of time on the part of senior executives, but it is likely one of their best investments. Creating alignment of direction is the most important work of leadership, and time invested here will pay off many times over.

Let us look at each of the questions a bit more closely.

1. *What* do we want to be?

In answering this question, leaders try to create clarity around the vision and mission of the business. A simple technique to use here is to brainstorm what it would look and feel like in a year or two when the leaders are done building the business or function the way they want to. When facilitating such a discussion for a leadership team, I ask them to imagine they are done setting up their business and that it is now functioning the way they wanted it to be. What does it look like? What does it feel like?

I capture their responses on a flip chart and request everyone not to critique anyone's idea—the idea here is to generate as many thoughts as possible. Typically, after about twenty minutes or so, the responses begin to converge and a theme begins to emerge. The responses then need to be cleaned up and a simple statement needs to be developed about the vision and mission.

Andy Grove ran Intel long before the company became one of the world's dominant producers of microprocessors. Before entering the microprocessor business, Intel was a leading manufacturer of memory chips. Legend has it that when Intel began to lose out in memory chips to low-cost manufacturers in Asia, he asked his senior team, "If the board brought in a new CEO, what do you think he might do?" "He would probably get us out of the memory business" came one reply. According to the story, Andy "symbolically" walked his team out of the room, then walked back in after a minute and said, "Let's get out of memories and figure out what we should do instead." And thus began the transition from manufacturing memory chips to microprocessors.

2. *Who* are our stakeholders?

a. What do we want to do for each?

Here, you go a step further and list each of the constituents the business or function wishes to serve. Are shareholders the one and only stakeholders or are there other constituencies as well? Clarity on *who* is very important. Without spelling it out, it is easy to neglect an important constituency. During my years at American Express, it was shareholders, customers, and employees. The company wanted to understand and spell out the needs of all three groups, and do the best job possible of addressing those needs.

In the short-term-oriented world of business, it is easy to focus just on shareholders or customers, thereby encouraging behavior and decisions that are not necessarily in the best long-term interest of the franchise. This is equally true if you lead an internal function like operations or information technology. You need to clearly articulate all your stakeholders and strike the right balance while addressing their needs.

When I was at American Express, each employee had to write down a set of goals for the year under each of the three categories. This goal-setting process started at the top of the company and was cascaded down throughout the company. Each employee received his or her manager's goals under the three categories—shareholders, customers, and employees—and wrote down their own goals to support their manager's overall goals. This simple but consistent process of goal setting created a line of sight through the whole company, and with this clarity, employees felt empowered to act in a way that best supported overall goals.

At Alibaba.com, Jack Ma repeatedly emphasizes that of the three main stakeholders, customers (the small and medium-size enterprises that the company serves) are the most important. Employees come second and shareholders third. Shareholder value is a function of creating customer value, and dedicated employees create customer value. At one of his annual general meetings, he famously told a crowd of shareholders that they (the shareholders) were last on his priority list after customers and employees, and that if they wanted shareholders to be first, they could go invest elsewhere. Ma was not trying to offend shareholders. His comments were based on his strong belief that shareholder value is a function of creating customer value, and dedicated employees create that customer value.

3. *How* will we get there?

    a. What is the conventional business model for our industry?

    b. What needs does the conventional model fulfill?

    c. What needs are yet unfulfilled?

    d. What new needs are likely to emerge in the future?

    e. What should we do differently compared to the traditional model?

Questions 1 and 2 ("what" and "who") defined your destination and stakeholders. Now you begin to shape your strategy, or how you plan to get there. The subquestions under question 3 here are self-explanatory. A leadership team or a strategy formulation group should go through each subquestion until a satisfactory answer is found. There is no fancy technique here other than careful data analysis and dialogue. Ultimately, the amount of rigor invested will determine how successful the strategy turns out to be. My suggestion here is that you make sure your team engages in this exercise. The idea of listing these questions is to give you a simple road map to guide your strategy formulation process. In my experience, many leaders take on a leadership position and dive straight into day-to-day problem solving. By the time they arrive at their new leadership position, a million things are already waiting for them, and it is "business as usual" in no time. However, I cannot overemphasize the need to step back from time to time and answer these questions.

The conventional business model for the credit-card industry is one of low cost and high volume. The idea is that a credit card is a commodity and that people do not want to pay much to own or use a card, and merchants want to pay the minimum possible fees. Visa and MasterCard were following this conventional model. Their goal was to increase volume—cards in force—and make their returns on volume rather than on margin. The conventional model filled the need for a convenient way to pay for purchases without carrying cash. It also fulfilled the need for low costs.

As American Express analyzed their options, they uncovered a new need for prestige. They believed that wealthy card members would be willing to pay a higher fee for better service and higher prestige. They also believed that merchants would welcome wealthy card members because they would spend more. While merchants will pay a higher commission to American Express, the expense will be more than offset by higher sales to the high-spending wealthy cardholders. So unlike the conventional model, the amount spent per card became an important variable, and margin rather than volume became the key metric.

Ultimately, American Express proved that if they followed a differentiated model built on prestige and high-quality service, focusing on the high-net-worth wealthy individual and the corporate community could be a highly profitable business.

When Jacqueline Novogratz and her team started the Acumen Fund, they were clear about the "what" and the "who." Acumen wanted to help meaningfully solve the problems of global poverty. They also knew that their main stakeholders were some of the poorest people in the world, on one hand, and philanthropic donors, on the other. However, they were less clear about the "how" and "why." Jacqueline was convinced that pure charity and aid was not the answer. According to her, while charity definitely meets some immediate needs, it also creates dependency, and fails to enable people to solve their own problems over the long term. Could there be a better approach to solving the problems of poverty? At the time, there were three main sources of capital—commercial (debt and equity), philanthropic (charity and aid), and micro-finance. While micro-finance was helping to some extent, it was not able to help those ventures where credit needs were greater than "micro," such as providing clean drinking water, disease prevention and control, and affordable housing.

Jacqueline and her team worked hard to find a solution, and ultimately designed an innovative solution called "patient capital." They would raise philanthropic capital like any other charity, but instead of just giving it away as needed to solve immediate problems, they would deploy it either as loans or as equity (as described in chapter 1) in ventures that were dedicated to solving such problems. It was called "patient" because Acumen would invest in such ventures for long periods of time and at below-market rates of return. By combining the essence of philanthropy with market-based commerciality, Jacqueline and her team were able to design an innovative approach to achieve their core mission.

4. *Why* will we succeed?

a. What will be our differentiating capabilities?

Once you have a strategy story, you need to make an honest assessment of your capability to deliver. What differentiating capabilities will your business need to succeed with the new strategy? Which of these do you already have? Of the ones you don't have, how will you get them? Will you build or buy?

Here you also clearly answer how you will make your returns: why will customers want to do business with you.

Harvey Golub and his team knew that exceptional service and the highest standards of integrity would be at the core of their strategy. They would make their returns by charging a premium for the exceptional service. To build this core capability throughout the company, the senior management team articulated a set of company values that they called the "blue-box values." I have seen many companies articulate values or business principles, but in most places they remain posters on the wall or modules in training programs. At American Express, they mattered. Because the values were so important to the success of the strategy, Harvey and his team created a compensation model that rewarded employees for living the blue-box values. Employees were encouraged in other ways, too, and the net result was the legendary American Express service. For example, stories of employees going above and beyond were highlighted on the company's Web site, and Harvey and his senior team often told those stories in their speeches.

For Howard Schultz at Starbucks, the key differentiators in his strategy were the quality of coffee and the experience (romance) of coffeehouses. After discovering the magic of coffeehouses in Milan, Howard was convinced that he could change the way people drank and enjoyed coffee in America, and charge a premium for providing the "experience." Many people questioned the soundness of his idea when he first tried to raise money to start his company. "Why would anyone pay a dollar and a half for a cup of coffee?" they asked. True to his vision, Starbucks has today become what Schultz calls the "third place" for people—a place other than home or office where people can visit or gather. Years later, in January 2007, while providing an update about the business on *The Charlie Rose Show,* he said, "Today, Starbucks serves over 40 million customers every week, we open six new stores somewhere in the world every day, we hire four hundred new people every day, and we have become the most frequented retailer in the world in which the core customer comes in about eighteen times a month." Forever the innovator, he went on to comment that despite the impressive growth, the story of Starbucks is still in its early stages.

Regardless of the size of your business or function, if you manage more than two layers of people, setting direction as described above is important for you as a leader. These are the brains of your business— the engine room of your ship. As they say, if you don't know where you're going, any road will get you there.

Once you've answered the four questions about your business, you need to articulate the story in a simple, concise, and powerful manner. If you cannot say it powerfully in fifteen minutes or less, or in fewer than two pages, it is not worth saying. Invest time up front in getting the communication right; it will save you lots of time later. You can use any format for communication that works for you, but follow the simple guidelines—fifteen minutes, and one to two pages. One method of doing this is using the one-page "what-who-how-why" template.

Essentially, the template requires you to state your objective (the "what"), list your stakeholders ("who"), and explain how you will succeed better than your competition or create something that does not exist ("how" and "why") all on one page. In fact, it allows you to show the "how" and "why" section in two ways, in a picture as well as in words. When we work with clients to help them use the template, they are often pleasantly surprised as to the extent of information that can be conveyed on just one page.

The best way to understand the template is to look at an example. In the 1980s and early 1990s, if American Express were to depict their strategy in the template format, my guess is it would look something like the figure on the facing page.

The top two boxes are self-explanatory. They simply state the core mission and the stakeholders served. The bottom ("how" and "why") box shows their strategy using a combination of a bar graph and bulleted text. The textured bars show choices made by the conventional model in order to meet stakeholder needs, and the solid bars show the American Express choices. The length of a bar toward the positive side shows the importance of each element to the business model, and the length on the negative side shows the extent of *un*importance. As you can see from the bar graph:

- The conventional model proposes very low cardholder fees, whereas Amex preferred a premium pricing strategy.

- The conventional model is based on revenue sharing. Issuers, networks, merchant banks, and merchant processors shared a

American Express Strategy

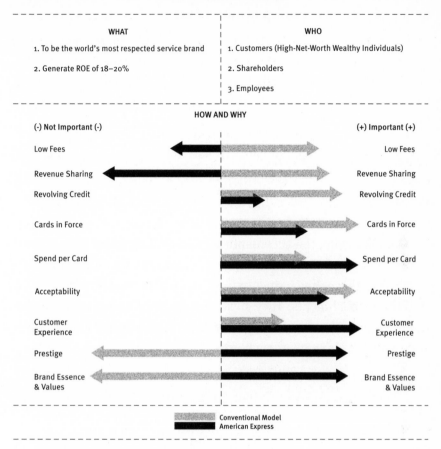

WHAT	WHO
1. To be the world's most respected service brand	1. Customers (High-Net-Worth Wealthy Individuals)
2. Generate ROE of 18–20%	2. Shareholders
	3. Employees

HOW AND WHY

(-) Not Important (-)   (+) Important (+)

Low Fees — Low Fees
Revenue Sharing — Revenue Sharing
Revolving Credit — Revolving Credit
Cards in Force — Cards in Force
Spend per Card — Spend per Card
Acceptability — Acceptability
Customer Experience — Customer Experience
Prestige — Prestige
Brand Essence & Values — Brand Essence & Values

Conventional Model
American Express

AMERICAN EXPRESS—STRATEGIC CHOICES AND ASSUMPTIONS

1. Premium pricing strategy

2. Own network, no revenue sharing with issuers and network providers

3. Essentially a charge-card business

4. Spend per Card is more important than Cards in Force (CIF)

5. Higher merchant commissions are more important than widespread acceptability

6. Superior customer experience and "prestige" will enable higher card-member fees

7. All employees must understand the essence of the brand and live the "Blue-Box Values"

piece of the pie. Amex deemphasized this feature and operated their own network and processing.

- Competitors using the conventional model largely made their money when cardholders revolved their payments, whereas Amex was essentially in the charge-card business, i.e., their cardholders paid their full balance at the end of each month.

- Cards-in-force (CIF) was the key metric for conventional competitors. The more cards in use, the higher the revenue. CIF was important to Amex, but not as much as it was to competitors. The amount each cardholder spent was more important.

- Because of the higher commission charged to member establishments, the acceptability of Amex was lower than that of Visa and MasterCard. Since Amex was targeting high-networth wealthy individuals who primarily shopped at premium establishments, they made a conscious decision to charge higher commission at the expense of wide acceptability. Strategy is about making choices.

- Competitors considered the credit card a utility. Customer experience and prestige did not feature as major factors in their business model. In a significant departure from the conventional model, American Express made customer experience a major focus of their strategy. Superior customer service, together with the prestige of owning a premium card, would allow Amex to charge higher fees. Since Amex cardholders were high spenders, establishments accepting the card were willing to pay a higher commission in return for the high spend.

- Unlike their competitors, Amex placed a major focus on internal factors such as individual job descriptions and culture (bones and nerves). Everyone attended intensive training on the essence of the American Express brand, and was fully aware what it meant to represent it. Through financial and nonfinancial means, employees were highly incentivized to protect and enhance the brand at any cost. Executives in leadership positions walked the talk about providing superior customer value while still driving best-in-class economics, and led by example. Harvey, along with his head of Human Resources at the time, Joe Keilty, created what were then called the blue-box values that everyone in the company was expected to live by.

- To support and encourage desired behavior, Joe and Harvey instituted a performance-management and reward system that measured and rewarded performance based on blue-box values. Each employee's performance was measured in terms of results against stated goals, as well as in terms of behavior against stated values. At the end of each year, all employees received a G/L performance rating where *G* stood for goals and *L* stood for leadership—living the values. On a rating scale of one to five where one was excellent and five was unsatisfactory, one could get the maximum possible bonus only if the performance rating was "1/1." If someone was a huge commercial producer (i.e., one on the G scale) but did not live the values to the fullest (i.e., three or four on the L scale), they would not be paid as much as someone with a "1/1" rating.

If this particular **what-who-how-why** template does not work for you, try something else. Another excellent methodology is the "strategy canvas," which can depict current, future, and competitors' strategy all on one chart, and forces teams to look for value innovation. Since the strategy is depicted in terms of a "value curve"—value that a business provides to its customers—it is easy to show differentiation between strategies. The methodology was developed by Renée Mauborgne and W. Chan Kim at the INSEAD business school, and is well laid out in their *Harvard Business Review* article titled "Charting

Your Company's Future" and in their bestseller *Blue Ocean Strategy*, published in 2005 by the Harvard Business School Press. While the strategy canvas does not allow for listing the objective, stakeholders, or strategic choices in words, what I like about it is its simplicity. It also provides an instant check for clarity. If your value curve is similar in shape to your competitors' curve, you know you need to work harder to find differentiation. Whichever template or tool you choose to use, the point is to keep refining your elevator speech until you can fit it neatly on one to two pages and say it within fifteen minutes or less. If you can say it in five minutes, that's even better.

In summary, the Brains (vision and strategy) are the backbone of any business. There are two keys to its success. First, the vision and strategy should be compelling and differentiated. Thoughtful analysis and focus on the **what, who, how,** and **why** questions can help ensure that this is the case. Second, communicating and cascading the strategy is as important as the strategy itself. The goal here should be to create so much clarity that everyone in the organization can consistently articulate vision and strategy. Adequate focus on the *Acceptance* (from $Q \times A = E$) is paramount.

If leaders do a good job at shaping and managing the brains of a business, employees throughout the organization should strongly agree with the following five statements:

1. We have a compelling vision for future success.

2. We have a clearly differentiated strategy to achieve our vision.

3. Vision and strategy are so clear that they guide resource allocation and decision making.

4. We have clearly recognizable core capabilities that give us our competitive edge.

5. Everyone in the organization can clearly and consistently articulate our value proposition to clients or customers.

I must emphasize here that this methodology of developing and communicating the "brains" is applicable to all levels of management, and to all functions including the back office. A department of just five people can use it as easily as a CEO and his direct reports. For junior and midlevel teams, it is an excellent way to communicate to superiors and get them on board with your ideas. For back-office teams that don't have competitors, you can use it to depict your "before and after" strategies, i.e., instead of showing the conventional business model, show the current way in which your department functions, and using a different color of bars, show the changes you propose to make in order to be more effective and efficient in the future. I have worked as a consultant with teams in all types of functions and businesses, including departments such as internal audit and operations. I have also used the methodology with central bankers and government departments. It works beautifully in all cases. Anyone who wants to develop a compelling strategy and communicate it powerfully can use it.

5

B-**B**-N: Building Strong "Bones"

Now that vision and strategy have been established, it is time to create an organizational framework that enables top-quality execution and long-term excellence. As stated earlier, doing so has two aspects— bones and nerves. "Bones" refer to the organizational design of the company, which should deploy resources in ways that best support the strategy. This is the formal organizational structure and the division of work among individuals and groups. "Nerves" are the informal setup, the culture of the organization. Bones create a structure for executing a strategy, and nerves create a culture that enables long-term excellence. In today's information age, technology or process can be copied in no time. Companies within an industry routinely poach talent from each other. The only sources of competitive advantage left are organizational architecture and culture—that intangible strength which enables a company to consistently perform at a higher level. When addressed proactively and thoughtfully, bones and nerves create conditions for sustainable, profitable growth. When handled poorly or not handled at all, they are a drag on overall performance. Businesses that fail to achieve their potential tend to do so more because of inadequate attention to bones and nerves, and less because of a lack of a good strategy. Most leaders eventually get their strategy right, but fail to execute or create long-term growth because of inadequate attention to bones and nerves.

DESIGNING THE ORGANIZATION TO EXECUTE THE STRATEGY (BONES)

Organizations should be designed and maintained such that employees can strongly agree with the following five statements:

1. We have top-quality talent with the right skills and experience in all key jobs.

2. Our supporting systems and structures (e.g., performance management, promotion processes) encourage desired performance.

3. Roles, responsibilities, and decision rights are defined as clearly as possible.

4. Our people and resources are deployed in a way that best supports the execution of our strategy.

5. The formal organizational structure enables the building and strengthening of our core differentiating capabilities.

To score highly on the above five factors of design, leaders need to first create an organizational structure that best serves flawless execution of strategy, then ensure each job is filled by the right person, and finally create supporting systems and processes that drive performance. All three are easier said than done, and despite all the right intentions, there are familiar traps that the most seasoned of executives fall into.

CREATING AN ORGANIZATIONAL STRUCTURE

Creating a structure for a business or a function within a large corporation is a sensitive subject because many people make decisions based on power and politics rather than actual business needs. Even though we live in the information and technology age, where important positions do not necessarily require numbers of people, compensation is still determined largely based on the "scope of position," i.e., the number of resources directly under the command of the position. Therefore most executives want more and more resources like head count and budget. In all my years as a consultant, I have yet to come across an executive who willingly gives up resources when he doesn't need them. My colleagues and I routinely facilitate executive teams in their efforts to transform the way they work. These transformation attempts stem from one of two situations—proactive or reactive. When a leader and his/her team undertake a proactive transformation, they assess how the world is changing around them, and discuss what they need to do differently to remain relevant. When the transformation exercise is in response to a cost-cutting initiative undertaken because of difficult market conditions, leaders focus on work that can be eliminated or reengineered in order to execute with a smaller head count and budget. In either case, at some point in the planning process, executives find themselves playing the turf-protection game. My favorite time during the discussions is when a senior executive says, "I don't have the resources to deliver on . . ." or "With this minuscule level of resourcing, we will only be able to do so much . . ." It is indeed interesting to watch the behavior of very senior executives when it comes to this point in the process. Most often, the level of resourcing is decided based on who has the maximum clout, rather than on what's best for executing the strategy.

In one situation, I was helping a group of senior HR professionals in their efforts to design a new organization structure that would allow them to save 40 percent in payroll costs. There were roughly 1,200 professionals in the global HR organization prior to the restructuring, serving a company of about twenty thousand people. Before the news of the restructuring was widely known, we conducted interviews to understand how work was done. We talked to over one hundred people in the HR organization globally, and each one complained about the inadequate level of resources they had. According to all of them, in order to execute everything on their plates, they needed more head count. Many talked about the danger of burnout and stress-related illness among the troops. Twelve hundred HR professionals serving a company of twenty thousand people means there was one HR person for every seventeen people. By any benchmarks, this was a large HR organization. Best-in-class ratios range from 100:1 to 150:1, and we were looking at 17:1. Yet everyone, including the senior HR team, was complaining about the lack of resources to do their work effectively. Furthermore, those who had relatively smaller teams were quick to complain about the "unjust" distribution of resources within the division. However, when we asked the business leaders they served, hardly anyone could articulate the value that the 1,200 HR professionals added to the business. Many were actually surprised that the HR group was so big.

Obviously there was a big disconnect here. The senior HR team was under the impression that they were working on extremely important mandates, but HR's clients—the business leaders and their teams that they served—were often at a loss to describe what HR actually did. Even if we make allowances for the fact that HR bashing is a favorite sport among business leaders, and even if we accept that a lot of the work HR does is invisible until something blows up, the numbers were not adding up.

While discussing how to go about meeting the challenge of designing a smaller organization while everyone was reporting a huge shortage of resources, I suggested that they do the following:

1. First, articulate a vision and strategy for what the new HR would deliver.

2. Next, list all current activities of HR and map them against the new strategy to see which ones were critical and which were not.

3. Based on step two, determine how many resources were decked against activities not considered critical in the strategy so that they could be eliminated.

4. Finally, determine the level of optimal resourcing required to execute the strategy, and make merit-based decisions to keep or let go of people until the reduction target was met.

The HR leaders in this case did a great job up to step three and into part of step four. The new strategy called for outsourcing routine processing work (like payroll and benefits administration) to a third party, and focusing HR's efforts on more strategic elements such as talent management and culture. However, when it became clear that even after eliminating noncritical tasks, they would still need to make cuts in order to staff the new organization, things became messy. When it came to assigning the number of boxes on organization charts, they decided primarily based on personal clout instead of going back to the drawing board and making further strategic choices. For example, when the head of HR for one of the most profitable divisions said recruiting was the most important HR function and therefore a large number of resources should be earmarked for recruiting, no one dared to challenge her because of her perceived close relationship with the CEO. When we suggested that they at least explore the option of having a dedicated contract with a reputed search firm instead of building up an in-house search function, the HR leader killed the discussion even before a meaningful dialogue could start. When they were finally finished, the HR organization was down to about 760 people, but no one felt upbeat about the new vision and strategy.

Even though the new plan was supposed to make HR more of a strategic partner to the business, the group failed to make the right choices and ended up retaining a lot of routine processing work that could have been outsourced. They also failed to agree upon beefing up strategic capabilities like in-house consulting and leadership development that could have positioned HR as a value-adding partner. Unlike many of our other clients who actually converted the threat of downsizing into a huge opportunity of accelerating future success, this particular HR group ended up with a suboptimal design based on interpersonal politics rather than on the strategy.

About six months after the restructuring, leaders and employees of the new HR organization were surveyed to find out how things were going. Again, everyone reported a severe lack of resources. Most people commented about the fact that resources had been taken away from them but the work had not gone away. Everyone wished they could revert to the old level of resourcing. I could not help but remember that they were saying the exact same things when they were a staff of 1,200. Does this story sound familiar? Even after what seemed like massive change, there was no improvement in overall impact. If you've lived within a large organization, regardless of the nature of business or geography, you will have indeed come across a situation not too dissimilar to this. The question is, why does it play out in this fashion in almost every business organization? The answer lies in the following basic insights:

> If the organizational structure is dictated by anything other than the business strategy itself, there is no framework for prioritizing work. Strategy is, after all, about making choices about what is important and what is not. In this sense, strategy provides a prioritization and decision-making framework. In the absence of an overarching framework for prioritization, sooner or later that organization will experience the all too familiar management trap—*too much to do, too few resources*. Without prioritization, how can you decide what work to cut or reduce?

> Unfortunately, this principle of designing an organization structure based on strategy is most often either forgotten or buried

under the weight of politics and turf protection. Money and head count are two resources that no one ever admits to having enough of; it is human nature to grab as much of them as possible.

At the end of the day, there is no perfect formula for determining the size and design of an organization. You have to look at your overall business strategy, make a few assumptions, and design an organization based on what is more or less important. For example, if the life-blood of the business is R&D, the question leaders must ask is, "Are we providing enough resources to this important function? If not, where can we reduce resources to fund this area?" When Neville Isdell started work on the turnaround strategy for Coke in 2005, it became clear that the company needed to increase its investment in marketing and new product development, the two areas that were most critical to the company. According to the company's 10K filings, between 2005 and 2007, expenditure on selling and general expenses rose significantly, largely due to an increased allocation for marketing, innovation, advertising, and selling expenses. Isdell prioritized the critical areas and restructured the company by putting as many resources in them as possible.

Once the initial design is completed, leaders must continue to fine-tune it until they get it almost right. Notice I said "almost" and not "perfectly" right. This is more art than science, and given that we are dealing with humans and not machines, there is hardly any chance of getting it perfectly right. And it's likely that by the time you get it almost right, your business model will have changed so much that you will need to go back to the drawing board. That's life in business. The fact is, organizational design is an ongoing task, not a onetime affair.

So the key point is to keep the big-picture strategy in mind while making resource allocation decisions. If something can be delivered with fewer resources, managers must willingly come forward and offer up resources under their control to areas that need them more. However, in reality most managers fashionably complain about the lack of resources in order to show how busy they are and how hard they are working. I often remind them that there are only two options—reprioritize, or justify an increase. In case of the latter, the mathematical logic (cost/benefit) should be clearly articulated. In some cases, this is easy to do. For example, in the financial advisory business, an increase in the number of financial advisers in the field directly corresponds to overall revenue and often profitability as well. In most cases, however, the justification is either weak or unclear. I often find that in the day-to-day pressures of work, people fail to look at the big picture and don't ask themselves if their resources are deployed most efficiently or not.

To address this problem, I ask my clients to list activities that don't take up a lot of resources but yield a disproportionately high level of commercial impact. I then ask them to list those activities that take up a lot of resources but do not yield an equivalent level of commercial impact. Next, I ask them to look at their current deployment model and determine how they should move their resources from low-yielding to high-yielding activities. After they get over their inevitable initial resistance, executive teams are generally very impressed with themselves at the end of this exercise because they always find ways to better deploy resources.

In one instance, we were working with the senior management team of a commercial bank. After we listed all the major activities of the bank alongside the number of resources each activity used, it became clear that a disproportionately large amount of resources were decked toward expanding the bank's branch network even while many branches were unprofitable. Further investigation revealed that since the bank's core segment was corporate banking, there was no positive correlation between the number of branch locations and successful growth in the corporate banking segment. Corporate clients were most interested in innovative and flexible funding and cash-management solutions, and did not care how many branches the bank had. Based on this analysis, the bank decided to cut down on the number of branches, and invest more in expanding the team of relationship managers who had expertise in commercial lending. To enable better cash-management services, the bank also decided to increase resources in their treasury department.

While many senior teams are able to make the right strategic choices as a result of the technique described above, it is extremely important to manage the communication process after decisions have been made. In my own management experience, I have often needed to reduce head count. No matter how much rigor you put into such an exercise, people who remain after a downsizing exercise feel pressured by the fact that a fewer number of them will now have to do all the work that was previously done by a larger number of people. The only thing that works in such situations is to carefully (and repeatedly) explain to people which parts of the strategy and business plan will now be deemphasized, and how you plan to refocus your resources in order to get the maximum impact. However good a job you do of explaining the new strategic focus, some people will invariably come to you and say, "I get the new strategy at a high level, but how will [this activity and that task] be done? Our clients still expect us to provide it." Faced with such push-back, leaders most often find themselves in a fix because they don't know how to answer the question. As senior leaders, they are now a bit removed from day-to-day work processes, so it is difficult for them to answer when challenged in this way. Here's something that always works.

Instead of trying to answer the question yourself, form a team of five to seven people who are closest to the work and ask them to solve the problem they raise to you. Task them to come up with recommendations about what to stop, start, and continue. The results are almost always amazing. The same group that felt helpless and overwhelmed a few weeks before now often comes back energized and excited about a plan that shows a way to have greater (not just the same as before) impact with fewer resources. This tactic of empowering people closest to the work to come up with solutions has never failed me.

At the end of the day, creating the right organization structure is like balancing your personal budget. Resources are always constrained, and balancing your personal budget is a matter of making strategic choices. Some people complain forever about not having enough money, and are therefore always unhappy with life. Others make choices about what is more or less important to them, and use their resources accordingly. They design their life based on their priorities, and find intrinsic happiness.

In the case of the HR organization I described earlier, the high head count was actually creating a problem. Everyone was trying to justify their existence by reinventing the wheel in their own silo instead of collaborating with colleagues and ensuring that best practices in one part of the company were adapted in other parts. Because there were so many HR people focused on very narrow aspects of work, the response time to HR's internal clients (the business leaders) was very slow. Too many people needed to get involved before HR could deliver something to a client. After they got past their successive reductions, clients actually reported that it was easier to get things done because there were fewer hurdles to jump.

Another simple technique to use while designing your organization's structure is to reverse-engineer your product or service-delivery model. This means mapping all the steps required to deliver your product and service to your customers and asking the questions:

1. How can we make this process more efficient?

2. Are there unnecessary layers of bureaucracy that we can remove?

3. Are there too many silos that slow us down?

4. Do decision rights sit in the right place? Are people empowered to do what is right for customers while still maintaining requisite standards? For example, if exceptional service is important, are customer service reps empowered enough to make decisions and delight customers?

Open and honest dialogue around these questions can help an organization in designing and improving its structure.

ENSURING THE BEST PEOPLE
FILL ALL KEY JOBS

Once an organizational structure is agreed on, jobs need to be filled with the best available talent. Here again, it is impossible to get all recruiting right the first time. No matter how much you try, some of your hiring decisions will prove to be wrong over time. So to get this right, the following tips should help:

- *Define performance expectations for each job.* Clarity around expected outcomes will highlight the skills and experience required for each job. If strategy has been laid out thoughtfully, this should not be difficult. Way too many people are hired every day without enough clarity on what is expected of them. The chances of success in such a case are limited. I have also seen the reverse, where too much detail is specified about a job and complex competency models are used to guide hiring.

Most competency models look at past success, and assume that what made someone successful in a similar job in the past will also make them successful in the future. But with the rate of change in the world today, such "look-back" models don't really hold true. Performance expectations should therefore be defined in terms of desired outcomes, not in terms of input. For example, if a job requires setting up and maintaining systems and structures for flawless execution of an aspect of strategy, the job description must list specific outcomes expected, such as production targets and quality measures. If the job requires creating new products or developing new markets, the description should include specifics, such as needs the new products must fulfill and the extent of market share required.

- *Hire for desired performance outcomes.* Instead of focusing on generic personality traits, look for evidence that suggests a person might have the skill and will to achieve the particular desired outcomes. I have seen many senior executives conducting interviews and making decisions based almost exclusively on gut feel, and many are proud of their "gut-feel" decisions. In one instance, I asked a senior leader after an interview what he thought of the candidate. "I liked him very much, we should hire him" came the prompt reply. When I probed deeper to find out what the leader actually liked about the person, he said he thought the candidate was a very nice person and it would be easy to work with him. I know this sounds too obvious as something not to do, but I cannot tell you how many decisions are made in this way rather than based on evidence of the required skill and will.

If job descriptions focus on expected outcomes as explained above, both the hiring manager and the candidate can make more informed decisions before filling a position. The hiring manager can probe the candidate for ideas on how they might go about achieving the outcomes, and the candidate can make a realistic assessment of his or her own capabilities and interest in working on those outcomes. Instead of describing expected outcomes, most job descriptions describe competencies and most hiring managers probe for past experience alone.

- *Be prepared to admit mistakes and rectify them.* As stated earlier, no matter how careful you are, hiring mistakes will happen. Once it becomes clear that a person you hired is a misfit for a particular role, you need to act quickly. You should either find them a role that might be a better fit for them or ask them to leave. This sounds harsh, but it is your job as a leader to ensure that all key jobs are staffed with the best people. Tolerating nonperformance sends the wrong signals to the rest of your organization, and overall performance level falls. When you ask leaders soon after they've let someone go if they did it too soon or too late, they almost always say too late. While it is hard to confront a person to tell them they need to go, it is the right thing to do both for the organization and for the individual. If you are convinced someone will not be successful in your organization, it is better to tell them sooner rather than later so they can find a job that is a better fit for them before it is too late.

It is unfair to let someone stagnate in a job because of mediocre performance and ultimately let them go at a later stage in life when they have greater family responsibilities such as college education expenses for kids. Telling someone early on in their career if they are not fit for the job at hand is the right thing to do because the incumbent still has the option of trying something different or learning new skills.

DESIGNING SYSTEMS AND PROCESSES THAT ENCOURAGE DESIRED BEHAVIOR

Once the organizational structure has been designed and the right people placed in key jobs as discussed above, appropriate systems and processes should be created to encourage desired behavior. Two important systems to think about here are the performance-management and promotion systems.

PERFORMANCE MANAGEMENT

It is said that what's measured gets done. Adequate thought must therefore be given to how performance will be measured. In most organizations, people are expected to achieve a set of commercial goals related to revenue, production, or processing. In addition, employees are also expected to live and behave according to the company's cultural values. However, most performance measurement systems measure performance only against commercial goals. To enable measurement of both commercial goals and values, individual performance must be defined on two levels: commercial goals and values.

At the commercial goals level, a manager and employee agree on *what* needs to be achieved during a performance period. At the values level, they agree on *how* it will be achieved. A simple example: Commercial goals specify a revenue, market share, service, or volume target. Values goals set guidelines for how to achieve those targets, e.g., by always keeping the customer's long-term interest in mind even when it means short-term loss of revenue. Another example of a values-based goal would be to coach and develop others. At most of the companies I have worked, besides being responsible for commercial production, each manager was also responsible for (and measured against) developing the people below them. Coaching people was an important part of the value system at these companies.

If you have a firmwide performance-management system, it should require all employees to establish goals and metrics at both levels—commercial goals and values. Once goals have been set, feedback must be exchanged throughout the year about performance against goals. Finally, at the end of the year, a formal performance evaluation must measure performance at both levels. Once employees know they will be measured for their values goals as well as their commercial ones, they will pay more attention to them.

During my time at American Express, performance was measured both against business goals and against leadership behaviors, which were described by way of thirteen leadership competencies such as setting direction, giving feedback, and listening to employees' concerns. The size of compensation (particularly bonus) depended equally on business goals and leadership performance, which made it abundantly clear to us that the company was serious about our leadership behavior or the lack of it. Just talking about values is not enough. It's important that performance be acknowledged with both financial as well as nonfinancial rewards such as public recognition of good behavior and positive feedback on performance. Nonfinancial rewards go a long way in reinforcing the culture, but are not enough in and of themselves. When used along with financial rewards, though, nonfinancial rewards are extremely effective.

PROMOTION

Almost everyone working for a large organization wants to be promoted at regular intervals. When they are up for promotion, employees are very receptive to feedback. This is an excellent time to reinforce the desired values. If someone is performing very well on commercial goals but not living the values enough, making promotion contingent upon improvement at the values level is an excellent tool to shape behavior. Many companies now require seeing a track record of values-based behavior before promoting people to key positions. This is easier said than done; typically, your biggest commercial producers show scant regard for values, and it is hard not to promote your cash cows for fear of losing them to competition. This problem is particularly acute in the banking industry. At the end of the day, this is where the rubber hits the road and leaders' seriousness of purpose is tested to the fullest.

A good way to deal with this dilemma is to let the commercial producers know they are being considered for promotion, but don't give it to them in the first year of consideration. Use the opportunity to explain to them why they did not make it, and help them to demonstrate desired behaviors in the following year. To reduce the chances of losing them to competition, pay them well that year and load up on deferred compensation. If they show noticeable improvement during the following year, promote them. Goldman Sachs does a particularly good job at this. People who are not "culture carriers" are typically given messages to that effect when they are due for a promotion, and are asked to demonstrate living the business principles before being eventually promoted. They are told that the firm values their commercial contribution, but for them to maximize personal success at the firm, they will need to do their share of firmwide activities such as recruiting, coaching, and training.

If designed in the manner described above, the bones will support overall vision and strategy in the best possible way. While getting this right is a matter of trial and error, keeping the basic principles of sound organization design—having the right people in key jobs, designing and maintaining a nimble and efficient organization structure, and establishing supporting systems like performance measurement—is helpful. If you are interested in a deeper look at these, I recommend reading any or all of the following books:

1. *Levers of Organization Design: How Managers Use Accountability Systems for Greater Performance and Commitment* by Robert Simons (Harvard Business School Press)

2. *Competing by Design: The Power of Organizational Architecture* by Michael Tushman and Mark Nadler (Oxford University Press)

3. *Designing Organizations: An Executive Briefing on Strategy, Structure, and Process* by Jay R. Galbraith (Jossey-Bass)

The role of organizational design is often underappreciated even though both strategy and culture depend on it. While brains, by way of vision and strategy, tell the organization *what to do,* and nerves, by way of a cultural ethos, tell an organization *how to behave,* it is the bones, the structure and supporting systems and processes, that *enable execution.* Adequate attention to this critical area is therefore a must. Leaders must keep an eye on the bones all year round and not delegate it to HR. Only senior leaders have the aerial view of the organization and only they can tell when the organization gets too siloed or complex. A periodic review of the effectiveness of the organization design should be built into a senior leadership team's management routines.

USING "BONES" TO DRIVE PRISON REFORM

Kiran Bedi, whom we met briefly in chapter 1, had the habit of creating something out of nothing, and of enabling positive change even in the most hopeless of situations. When she arrived at the Tihar Jail in New Delhi on her first day of duty as inspector general of prisons, she was horrified. Anyone in her place would have been horrified considering the conditions she inherited. There was an extremely foul stench permeating the sprawling campus because tons of garbage lay everywhere, with human waste unflushed in toilets and in open drains everywhere. Water was an extremely scarce resource. The situation was particularly bad during the monsoon months, when a phenomenon called "reverse flow" occurred. Thanks to the rain, the contents of clogged sewers would flow back into prisoner barracks, causing even more stench, filth, and rampant disease. The campus, made up of four prisons, was built to hold about 2,300 inmates, but it housed almost ten thousand. To say that conditions were inhuman would be a gross understatement.

From the worst-quality food to widespread corruption and violence, the world inside the high walls of the prison campus was one in which life had become degraded beyond imagination. Senior officials in charge of the prison system rarely visited the campus, and prison staff was both de-motivated and corrupt. They felt threatened by the hardened criminals and often resorted to merciless beatings of prisoners, and connived with gang lords. To get even the basics like medical supplies for the sick, prisoners had to bribe officials or curry favor.

Women were perhaps the worst off. When one British inmate asked for help with visitor rights, she was told that one never gets anything for nothing, and that if she wanted to exercise her rights, she would have to grant sexual favors. Prison staff had long given up any semblance of morality or ethics. Women prisoners were routinely made to stand behind the gates of the prison, and staff collected money from men outside for the privilege of fondling the women through the bars of the gate . . . Such was the extent of degradation of the system!

What was Kiran going to do? Most of her predecessors had employed the same coping strategy—turn a blind eye, become a part of the corruption, and enjoy the benefits. It was easy to blame the "system" for the conditions. "After all," they reasoned, "what happens inside the prison is a microcosm of life outside. The whole country is corrupt, and nothing can be done." I asked Kiran to recount her early thoughts on arriving at Tihar, and here's what she said: "They [the higher-ups] had sent me to Tihar to lock me up. They wanted to break my will. I had already created enough trouble for them, and they did not want me running to enlist the media's help on yet another of my harebrained community service ideas. They thought sending me to Tihar would be the ultimate fix. But as always, I asked myself what my overall mission was, and I reminded myself that above all else, I wanted to make a difference and make the world a slightly better place. I then asked myself how my current assignment fit in with my mission, and the answer was clear to me. This place needed leadership more than any other place. If I could make even a small difference in restoring dignity and hope, perhaps the prisoners and staff would do something positive." While describing her first day in the prison, she said, "I decided to take a walk inside one of the prison wards to see things for myself. I had decided to dress in civilian clothes that day because I wanted to establish a connection with the prisoners based on empathy rather than authority. I wondered if our criminal justice system were at all fashioned to help change offenders and forgive those willing to mend. Taken aback by the blank stares around me, I asked the prisoners, 'Do you pray?' No one answered, and they continued to stare at me hopelessly. I raised my voice and asked again, this time in Hindi. Ultimately one of the men replied in the affirmative. I continued to ask until most of them joined in with a yes. I then invited them to close their eyes and sing a prayer with me. I chose a song that praised and thanked the Lord, but did not belong to any particular faith. It was a popular Hindi film [Bollywood] song, so most prisoners were familiar with it. We all closed our eyes and sang together. When I opened my eyes, I knew we had succeeded in giving out the first signal of mutual trust, which would set the pace of our working relationship from then on."

Listening to her, I couldn't help thinking to myself that this was the same woman who had single-handedly fought a mob of about a hundred armed men, and who was routinely called "supercop" by the media largely because of her courage. It was great to see both extremes—strength and compassion in the same person.

Kiran knew she needed to make serious changes. She saw two different yet interconnected issues: One was the quality, motivation, and conduct of her staff; the second was the condition of the prison inmates themselves. She decided to address the former first and called an all-staff meeting. She was surprised to learn that this would be the first time that staff from all four prisons had ever gotten together.

Kiran knew that she had been thrust upon them and that their strategy would be to somehow suffer her until she was transferred to her next posting. But she also knew that the staff needed healing. They needed a leader. As she talked to them, it became clear to her that they were scared of the gangsters and hardened criminals in their midst. The criminals regularly threatened the staff with dire consequences and physical harm to their families if they did not comply with their demands, and the residential compound in which staff families lived did not have a security system or guards to protect the families. In continuing the dialogue with her staff, she learned that their needs were basic. They wanted to be heard, they wanted security for themselves and their families, they wanted to be appreciated, and above all, they wanted a meaningful purpose. With a few exceptions, most staff members wanted to go back home each night to their families feeling a sense of achievement and respectability. No one had ever heard them, and their own insecurities were driving them to behave in brutal and inhuman ways with prisoners.

By any measure, the prison was understaffed. Add to that the lack of skill and will, and it was clear that this was hardly the army that could achieve anything, let alone the remarkable transformation Kiran had in mind. But despite the quality of people at her disposal, Kiran knew she had no choice but to use the staff she had. The authorities above her would never listen to her plea for more (and better) resources. While I have talked at length about getting the right people in key jobs, it is not always possible to do this. In some cases, you have to play the hand dealt to you. Kiran had to get the best out of the staff she had. By probing and listening, she understood the needs of her staff and began addressing them. She built a wall around the residential compound, appointed security guards, and allowed officers to keep weapons at home for their self-defense. She then invited them to join her in reforming the prison campus by inviting their suggestions. It was clear that they were eager to participate.

Through a process of collective brainstorming, Kiran and her team developed a vision: to transform the Tihar hellhole into an "ashram," which in Hindi means a place for learning and healing. "Why ashram?" I asked her. She answered: Earlier, their time in prison did not teach inmates anything. In fact, the only thing they did while in prison was to make plans to commit more crime. While leaving the prison, they promised to return to their fellow-inmate friends soon. The only friends they had were in the prison. Our goal was to give them skills and self-esteem to go back into society as meaningful participants. When the transformation was well under way, there was a slogan among the inmates: "We will leave here never to return." For the first time in its history, the Tihar Jail had a stated mission and goals and objectives to achieve the mission.

To make it all possible, Kiran began an extensive training and development program to upgrade the skills and knowledge of her staff. Again for the first time, prison staff felt invested in, and learning became a habit. Through a disciplined management routine involving regular meetings to monitor progress, Kiran began the transformation of Tihar. While the staff now had a new sense of meaning, and was motivated to perform at a higher level, the shortage of resources remained a big problem. To reform a place as degraded as Tihar, many more resources were needed. Kiran had been in such situations before, and knew very well that asking the government for help would be a waste of time. She had to find innovative ways to get what she needed. This is when she did what had never been heard of before: She turned to the prisoners themselves, and invited them to join the process. "If our goal was to reform rather than to punish prisoners, if our goal was to send them out of here as responsible citizens, how could we not involve them in the process?" said Kiran in response to my question about how she decided to use the prisoners in the reform revolution. "We were looking for a solution to our biggest problem—the lack of resources—and then we realized that the answer had been in front of us all along. It was the human resources of the prison itself," she added.

Taking her cue from the *panchayat* system, a system of self-governing citizen councils in rural India, Kiran and her senior staff created several councils to address the most pressing problems of the prison, and invited prisoners to fill positions on them. She explained that the main objective was to encourage prisoners to voluntarily take part in organizing educational, cultural, and sports activities, and also to maintain discipline. Before the formation of the various *panchayats* (councils), jail officials conducted orientation programs for inmates to explain the workings and benefits of the new system. Self-management was the new name of the game at Tihar. A total of twelve *panchayats* were formed, including ones concerned with literacy, medical, and legal services. Inmates, who until that point had only received poor food, regular beatings, and brutal treatment from prison staff and fellow prisoners, began to teach, oversee the improvement of food quality, and provide legal aid to the thousands of people being tried. To everyone's surprise, with the exception of just a handful of inmates, all the inmates willingly participated in these initiatives. For the first time, they saw a ray of light in an otherwise hopeless existence.

The performance of each *panchayat* was measured and members were held responsible for results. The results achieved by the legal aid council were particularly impressive. It was led completely by inmates with legal backgrounds, and in 1994, a total of 641 petitions were filed on behalf of prisoners: 354 received relief. In the past, the only way to file appeals and petitions was to go through lawyers from the outside. More often than not, these lawyers took advantage of the lack of education among the accused, and extorted money from them without providing adequate service. Now inmates could get quality legal aid without spending money. Court fees and other legal expenses were paid from the prisoners' welfare fund, which earned its revenue from goods and services that prisoners produced and sold outside the prison.

The transformation of Tihar, achieved in less than two years, was remarkable. I asked Kiran to tell me about the long-term impact of her work there, and she recounted several stories of inmates who had carried on the work they had learned at Tihar after being released. Most important of all, with the help of the Human Rights Commission, the transformation of Tihar from a place of terror and punishment to a place of reform and renewal received the attention of the government, and the 1894 Prisons Act was revised to incorporate the continuation of practices started at Tihar.

Kiran finally retired from active police duty in 2009 to focus fully on the nonprofit organizations she heads. In a 2010 *Reader's Digest* poll, she was ranked first among women, and third among all Indians, on the list of the most trusted people in India. Throughout her career, she managed to create something out of nothing, often by creating strong "bones" even in the most difficult of conditions. I asked her why some leaders manage to achieve so much despite everything, while others, even while they have powerful resources at their disposal, achieve little or nothing, and she made a powerful point. First, she believes leaders should be net givers, not primarily takers. "By appointing them to a leadership position, society has already rewarded leaders with respect and power. Now they must give back to society by creating positive change in a selfless way. The problem is, most people remain net takers and never become givers. And as long as you remain a net taker, you cannot create positive change," she said.

6

B-B-N: Developing Cultural "Nerves"

Take a look at the following pairs of companies:

1. Goldman Sachs/Lehman Brothers

2. Pepsi/Coca-Cola

3. Toyota/General Motors

What are the similarities within each pair? Each was a top name in their industry for a considerable length of time. Each was a fierce competitor in the marketplace. Both hired similar people, developed similar products, and deployed similar technologies to serve their customers. Yet the long-term financial performances of each company in the pairs tell a very different story. Based on historical price data, if you owned shares of Goldman Sachs and Lehman Brothers between May 1999 and May 2009, your Goldman investment would have appreciated by 92.55 percent, whereas your Lehman investment would have depreciated by 99.71 percent. If you owned shares of Coca-Cola and Pepsi between April 1999 and April 2009, your Pepsi investment would have appreciated by 42.08 percent, whereas your Coke investment would have depreciated by 22.60 percent. Finally, if you owned shares of Toyota and General Motors between April 1999 and April 2009, your Toyota investment would have appreciated by 38.68 percent, whereas your GM investment would have depreciated by 98.34 percent.

In an age in which technology and information are no longer considered competitive advantages, what happened here? A detailed analysis would certainly reveal a number of specific reasons for the gaps in financial performance, but these examples (and a host of others) also point toward one major differentiator—culture. Over years of consulting and talent-management work, I have found that if managed proactively and effectively, culture can be a big source of competitive advantage. Look at Goldman Sachs and Lehman Brothers over the past ten years. Both recruited from top colleges around the world, compensated their employees competitively, offered the same products and services to their clients, and operated in the same market cycles. If there were one overarching difference between the two, it was the way they managed culture.

THE GOLDMAN DIFFERENCE

Culture evolves whether you do anything about it or not. At Goldman, where I spent six years, senior leaders took culture very seriously. Teamwork wasn't just a slogan, it was a reality. In fact, lone stars did not survive too long at Goldman; everyone naturally helped everyone else. What mattered most was that the firm succeeded against competitors. If you wanted information about a client or a project you were working on, you could leave a voice-mail message to a bunch of fellow colleagues around the firm, and you would most definitely have responses in eight hours or less, irrespective of time-zone differences.

Ask anyone at Goldman what makes him or her so successful year after year and he or she will invariably reference "strong culture." That said, strong cultures have a dark side as well, and need to be constantly managed in order to avoid negative consequences. Leaders of companies with such strong cultures need to be ever vigilant about the danger of overusing the strengths of their culture. When overused, the strengths can easily become liabilities. This was evident in the aftermath of the 2008 subprime mortgage crisis at Goldman, when some parts of the firm forgot the firm's long-held business principles and became overzealous about maximizing shareholder returns and creativity, perhaps at the expense of putting clients first, and integrity.

Such stray incidents notwithstanding, Goldman was (and still is) very particular about how they recruit and how they promote. In both cases, a huge amount of emphasis is placed on the question of cultural fit: Does this person believe in and live the cultural values of the firm? At Goldman, if you are not a "culture carrier," you do not have a bright future.

Decisiveness is another notable feature of Goldman's culture. Goldman espouses the principle "Debate Freely, Decide Swiftly." While input is sought from a variety of people on important issues, decisions are made quickly. And once a decision is made, everyone gets behind the decision even if initially opposed. A strong 360 feedback system ensures that people support and respect each other. Every employee participates in the annual 360-degree review exercise, which asks questions about the employee's behavior against the firm's business principles. A unique feature of Goldman's annual review system is that it does not ask the question, Did the individual achieve stated performance goals? Excellent performance is a given; it is what earns you the right to your continued role within the company. The review system tries to assess *how* you work, and if you "live" the cultural values or not, by asking questions like whether or not the employee is a team player. If someone receives negative feedback about teamwork, respect for others, decisiveness, etc., she gets paid less than what she could have potentially earned in that year. If negative feedback becomes a pattern, it generally leads to separation from the firm.

That Goldman had a strong culture of leadership and respect became clear to me early in my tenure there. I had moved from India to the United States with American Express; two years later Goldman offered me a job in Hong Kong. They wanted a world-class learning and development function in Asia, and wanted me to take the job. My wife and I had wanted to live in New York, so I was hardly keen on the transition. However, after twelve years at American Express, I was ready for the next challenge and agreed to take the job, operating on the condition that the firm would relocate me back to New York after two years. We agreed that I would set up the department, find and groom a successor, and hand over the reins at the end of two years. However, as the two-year period was drawing to a close, the bull-market period during which I was hired had given way to the famous dot-com crash and subsequent bear market in 2001–2002. There were no jobs in New York to come back to.

Around this time, Kevin Kennedy, a long-standing senior partner of the firm, an investment banker for thirty years, was named the head of the Human Capital Management (HCM) division. I was still discussing the issue of my possible return to New York with my immediate superiors when Kevin made a trip to Hong Kong. The purpose of his visit was one-on-one meetings with key senior HCM directors, and I was one of them. I will never forget our first meeting.

He walked into my office and sat down on a chair in front of my desk. I asked him what part of the business he would like to hear about, to which he responded, "Let's get straight to the point. We pulled you out of a great job at American Express less than two years ago, uprooted your family from a nice life in New York, you came here and did a bang-up job for us based on a commitment we made, and now the kids want to go back home, right?"

I was speechless. I had been thinking for days about how to broach this subject with him without offending my immediate managers. He had taken the trouble to find out all about me; he had determined how I was "wired," or premotivated, and it seemed he was determined to do what was right. He then went on to ask me what job I wanted in New

York, and eventually said, "Find a successor, get him or her settled in, and come see me when you arrive in New York. And since I am sure you have nothing else you want to discuss with me at this time, with your permission, I'd like to end this meeting right here so I can get a break before my next one." With that, he got up and walked out!

Needless to say, this was decisive leadership at its best: Goldman's greatness at work. Yes, the economy was tough; yes, there was no immediate job for me in New York; and yes, I should have been grateful for having any job in that market instead of fussing about a commitment. All of this was true. However, Kevin hit upon a greater truth—a leader should do whatever he can to keep a good employee happy, and trust in commitments is a significant part of that equation. Kevin had no hesitation in making the decision because he was operating under Goldman's strong culture based on the fourteen business principles I touched upon earlier.

At Goldman, you can touch and feel the tenets of their philosophy:

1. Our clients' interests always come first. Our experience shows that if we serve our clients well, our own success will follow.

2. Our assets are our people, capital and reputation. If any of these is ever diminished, the last is the most difficult to restore. We are dedicated to complying fully with the letter and spirit of the laws, rules and ethical principles that govern us. Our continued success depends upon unswerving adherence to this standard.

3. Our goal is to provide superior returns to our shareholders. Profitability is critical to achieving superior returns, build-

ing our capital and attracting and keeping our best people. Significant employee stock ownership aligns the interests of our employees and our shareholders.

4. We take great pride in the professional quality of our work. We have an uncompromising determination to achieve excellence in everything we undertake. Though we may be involved in a wide variety and heavy volume of activity, we would, if it came to a choice, rather be best than biggest.

5. We stress creativity and imagination in everything we do. While recognizing that the old way may still be the best way, we constantly strive to find a better solution to a client's problems. We pride ourselves on having pioneered many of the practices and techniques that have become standard in the industry.

6. We make an unusual effort to identify and recruit the very best person for every job. Although our activities are measured in billions of dollars, we select our people one by one. In a service business, we know that without the best people, we cannot be the best firm.

7. We offer our people the opportunity to move ahead more rapidly than is possible at most other firms. Advancement depends on merit, and we have yet to find the limits to the responsibility our best people are able to assume. For us to be successful, our men and women must reflect the diversity of the communities and cultures in which we operate. That means we must attract, retain and motivate people from many backgrounds and perspectives. Being diverse is not optional; it is what we must be.

8. We stress teamwork in everything we do. While individual creativity is always encouraged, we have found that team

effort often produces the best results. We have no room for those who put their personal interests ahead of the interests of the firm and its clients.

9. The dedication of our people to the firm and the intense effort they give their jobs are greater than one finds in most other organizations. We think that this is an important part of our success.

10. We consider our size an asset that we try hard to preserve. We want to be big enough to undertake the largest project that any of our clients could contemplate, yet small enough to maintain the loyalty, intimacy and the esprit de corps that we all treasure and that contribute greatly to our success.

11. We constantly strive to anticipate the rapidly changing needs of our clients and to develop new services to meet those needs. We know that the world of finance will not stand still and that complacency can lead to extinction.

12. We regularly receive confidential information as part of our normal client relationships. To breach a confidence or to use confidential information improperly or carelessly would be unthinkable.

13. Our business is highly competitive, and we aggressively seek to expand our client relationships. However, we must always be fair competitors and must never denigrate other firms.

14. Integrity and honesty are at the heart of our business. We expect our people to maintain high ethical standards in everything they do, both in their work for the firm and in their personal lives.

CULTURE—THE REAL THING

Phrases like "a culture of excellence" or "winning culture" have, of course, become standard fare in management circles. Nowhere else was this more pronounced than at Coca-Cola in the eighties and nineties under Roberto Goizueta, who made winning an obsession all across the company.

Goizueta was the CEO from August 1980 until his untimely death in October 1997, and under his direction, Coke went from strength to strength, further solidifying its position as a top U.S. corporation. He is known for invigorating the company with a compelling vision and a strong positive culture of excellence. In the process, he created more shareholder wealth than any other CEO in history until that time. But after his death, under the stewardship of two successive CEOs with a vastly different leadership style and philosophy, the company experienced turbulence on many fronts, including accusations of rigging a marketing test for frozen Coke in 2000, as a result of which the company admitted to wrongdoing by some employees and agreed to pay $20 million to Burger King and its associates; SEC investigations for overstatement of financial results; and a $192.5 million settlement for a race bias case. Ultimately, in June 2004, Neville Isdell, a longtime Coke veteran, was asked to return to the company as its leader.

Isdell did what any good leader would do: He formulated a new strategic direction for the company, and began rebuilding the old culture of excellence. Under his leadership in 2005, the company published its "Manifesto for Growth," a booklet that clearly laid out a course for rebuilding. The booklet was made available to all employees and also to anyone outside the company who wanted it. In spite of the fact that the document was readily shared with people inside and outside the company, it admitted failings in recent years, including the fact that Coca-Cola had lacked clear direction and a common understanding of purpose as a company. The booklet also acknowledged the fact that the company had become reactive and fragmented, and as a result was not achieving its true potential in the market. After openly admitting and accepting reality, the booklet went on to talk about the fact that the company would re-create its brilliance and become a responsible and successful company again, and laid out a plan to do so.

In order to achieve the sustainable growth the manifesto talked about, six growth paths were identified. To execute these paths, the company set out to create a culture of six distinctive capabilities, such as marketing, franchise leadership, and people development, and seven core values to guide behavior. As I was considering an offer to join Coca-Cola in late 2005, I was impressed by the fact that the company had the courage to accept reality and admit some mistakes in an openly available document—the manifesto. Second, there was no doubt that culture was seen as an important vehicle for growth. By the time I joined the company in February 2006, the manifesto was in full execution mode. The results of Isdell's leadership were soon clearly visible. Business performance began to improve in almost every area of the company. On January 17, 2006, the stock price (KO) was $40.09. By January 7, 2008, it had reached $63.77. Clearly, the company was well on its way to undoing past mistakes and solidifying its position as a growth company once again. A large part of the turnaround can be attributed to the grassroots-level capability and culture building that Isdell initiated.

Coke is once again competing formidably with archrival Pepsi. Here was another strong culture that had momentarily lost its way until Isdell helped find it again. Unfortunately, such a turnaround did not happen with the once mighty General Motors, which ultimately handed over global leadership of the auto industry to Toyota.

KAIZEN CULTURE

The story of Toyota and General Motors is familiar to most people. Toyota's culture is defined by its strong focus on quality. Google the words "Toyota Culture" and you find hundreds of articles and books crediting the company's sustained success to its culture of high performance and to kaizen, which means "continuous improvement." At Toyota, constantly challenging oneself to find better ways of doing things is a way of life. If an assembly-line worker notices any problem, he or she is given the liberty to stop the production line. Because problems are seen as opportunities for better solutions, everyone exposes them. According to David McBride in his 2004 article titled "Lean Culture: The Toyota Culture of Continuous Improvement," Toyota employees generate over one million process improvement ideas every year. Of these, over 90 percent get implemented. I know many companies that invite suggestions from employees, but have never come across one that comes anywhere near the 90 percent implementation rate. Toyota's senior management has actively created this culture.

Yes, Toyota has had quality problems of late. However, even in fiscal 2009—the year in which the company recalled more than 8.5 million cars worldwide—it has declared a profit of $1.2 billion, and has forecast a profit of $3.3 billion for 2010. Even the world's best companies make mistakes. While the storm is far from over, the key issue for sustainable success concerns the strength of the culture and its ability to recognize its own mistakes in a timely manner, and to course-correct. So far, Toyota is showing that it can. Consumers seem to agree. According to a *Wall Street Journal* article dated May 12, 2010, in the United States—where most of Toyota's problems are centered—it has regained 16 percent market share in 2010 despite regular negative headlines in local and national dailies. The article also quotes an Automotive Lease Guide survey of U.S. consumers released in March 2010 that showed that 67 percent of respondents weren't affected by the recall or that they had a positive view of Toyota's response.

In an article entitled "How Toyota Is Rejuvenating the Idea of Corporate Culture," Antoine Henry de Frahan writes about how Toyota competes with itself. In his estimation, Toyota is "obsessed with self-criticism, there is a healthy, however pervasive, paranoia about the future; a lack of complacency when it comes to past achievements."

Another aspect of Toyota's culture, Frahan conjectures, is disdain for disruptive reorganizations as a way to create change: "Toyota doesn't have corporate convulsions, and it never has. It restructures a little bit every work shift. Continuous improvement is tectonic. By constantly questioning how you do things, you don't outflank your competition next quarter. You outflank them next decade."

GM, as we knew it, could not be more different. In a recent issue of *Fortune,* Steven Rattner, the head of the auto task force appointed by President Obama in the aftermath of the global recession, writes, "Everyone knew Detroit's reputation for insular, slow-moving cultures. Even by that low standard, I was shocked by the stunningly poor management that we found, particularly at GM." According to Rattner, top executives at GM's headquarters kept their communication and contact with employees to a minimum. They were housed on the uppermost floor of the building behind locked and guarded glass doors, and had special elevator cards that allowed them to descend to their private garages without stopping on any other floors. "In my relatively few interactions with chairman and CEO Rick Wagoner, I found him to be likable, dedicated, and generally knowledgeable. But Rick set a tone of 'friendly arrogance' that seemed to permeate the organization," he adds.

According to Bill Vlasic, writing for the *New York Times,* in the old days, the evaluation of GM employees was based on a performance measurement process that could fill a three-ring binder. It is ironic that while the company was constantly losing market share and failing to deliver on its quality promises, employees were measured so thoroughly. What were they measuring? After the company emerged from bankruptcy, the system was replaced by a simple one-page performance appraisal. "For all its financial troubles and shortcomings" writes Vlasic, "no aspect of GM has confounded its critics as much as its hidebound, command and control corporate culture."

Unlike Toyota, where every assembly-line worker is empowered to halt the line if he has an idea to make something better, at GM any changes to a product program needed to be reviewed by as many as seventy executives, often taking months before a decision could be made. According to Vlasic, in 1988, when GM still dominated the U.S. market, a senior executive named Elmer Johnson wrote a strong memo highlighting GM's inability to execute in a timely manner. As expected, the memo fell upon deaf ears—because the culture emphasized past glories and current market share rather than focusing on the future.

The examples above, and many others I have seen over the years, point to an indisputable fact: You need to manage culture proactively. I have heard many management experts talk about culture. They all concur that changing a culture or creating one from scratch is extremely difficult. Most go on to say that it takes anywhere from five to ten years before a culture can change in a meaningful way. I respectfully disagree, because I believe it is neither difficult, nor does it takes that long. Creating or changing a culture is more about seriousness of purpose on the part of business leaders, and less about management techniques or "change initiatives." I have seen many companies spend millions on external consultants and launch several misguided "culture-change" initiatives. I have seen others delegate culture to Human Resources. These efforts don't succeed because the work of creating and maintaining a culture cannot be delegated.

Proactive management of culture is a primary task of leadership, and only if leadership walks the talk and leads from the front does a culture take hold. In the following pages, I will introduce a simple process that leaders can use to change a culture or establish a desired culture. I will offer a basic definition of corporate or organizational culture, and then suggest a simple but powerful way of creating it.

ESTABLISHING
THE CULTURE ADVANTAGE

On 9/11, when the planes hit the World Trade Center, the CEO of a big U.S. technology company was on a plane to Asia. When she heard the news upon landing, she immediately tried to get in touch with her office in California, but thanks to the jammed phone lines and the sixteen-hour time difference, it was several hours before she could get through to her senior team. When she did get them on a conference call, she laid out three immediate priorities for them:

1. Immediately account for every employee and ensure they are all safe

2. Ensure that the company's Web site and servers—the core of their business—are secure

3. Begin organizing a charity auction in order to support victims and their families

After a brief silence on the other end of the line, someone in the conference room informed the CEO that the three priorities had not only been identified, the first two had already been completed and the third was well on its way. I cannot remember where I heard this story, but it makes a strong point: This was the company's culture at work!

For a business leader, a simple way of looking at your organization's culture is: *Culture is what your people do when no one is looking.*

This is an important definition because as organizations grow in size and complexity, it is simply impossible to monitor day-to-day individual performance. Even if it were possible, it would be an extremely inefficient use of the leader's time. Once strategy and objectives are set, it is important that employees conduct themselves every day in a way that helps achieve those objectives. If employees pull in different directions based on their own individual understanding of what to do or not do under different circumstances, the chances of that organization achieving its strategic objectives are next to none. So as leaders, you need a mechanism that ensures that people do the right thing every day, even when no one is looking. At the end of the day, you have to clarify performance expectations, create conditions that enable success, and trust that people will behave in a way that best supports overall strategy. This is where culture comes in. To repeat, culture is what people do when no one is looking. In companies like American Express, customer service is so deeply ingrained in the culture that employees automatically know what to do when a customer has a problem.

Here is another example of culture at work. I am an Indian citizen but started living in the United States in 1998. Barring a couple of short stints overseas, New York has been home ever since. However, I make it a point to visit India at least once a year. Driving back to our family home late one night after dinner with some friends in New Delhi, I stopped at a red light. Before I knew it, the car behind me started honking, urging me to keep going. I ignored the honking and continued to wait for the light to turn green. Frustrated with me, the driver of the car behind pulled up next to me, rolled down his window, and angrily asked me why I was blocking his way. When I pointed toward the red light, he yelled at me for being stupid enough to care about red lights at 1 a.m. when there was hardly any traffic on the road, and drove off in a huff. I could not help but think to myself that this was culture at work again—*culture is what your people do when no one is looking!* Back in the United States, most people don't even think about driving through a red light no matter what time it might be or how empty the road might be. I am not making a case for right or wrong here: I am just trying to demonstrate a point about culture at work.

So how do you go about creating the culture you want? The first condition is to strongly believe in the cultural philosophy you espouse as a leader. Only embark on creating a culture if you are strongly convinced that it is critical for success. Most culture-change efforts fail because leaders themselves lack conviction. If you don't believe in what you say, sooner or later people find out. "Be the change you want to see in the world," Gandhi said. There is no substitute for genuine leadership and seriousness of purpose. For example, if you want all your employees to openly admit mistakes, you as a leader must believe in the idea and be willing to role-model it. I do not have a standard profile of a high-performance or winning culture to share because there is no such thing. Leaders of an organization must decide how they want their employees to behave and how they want customers and other stakeholders to experience the organization. Asking the question, What kind of culture will best enable us to achieve our strategic objectives? is also a good place to start. Once you are fully convinced about the change you want to bring about in your culture, you need to follow three simple steps—*define, socialize,* and *reinforce*—and then stay focused on them relentlessly.

Creating a Culture of Excellence

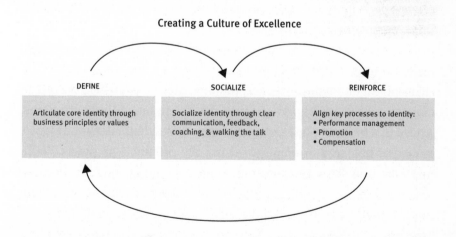

DEFINE	SOCIALIZE	REINFORCE
Articulate core identity through business principles or values	Socialize identity through clear communication, feedback, coaching, & walking the talk	Align key processes to identity: • Performance management • Promotion • Compensation

DEFINE—SOCIALIZE—REINFORCE

DEFINE

The first step is to define the desired culture. Here, leaders articulate a set of behavior guidelines for everyone to follow. A simple way of determining such guidelines is to engage in the following exercise.

Imagine it is a year or two from the time the vision and strategy were set. Imagine also that the new strategic direction was executed flawlessly and the organization has been very successful in meeting its stated objectives. With this backdrop, list behaviors that made this success possible. Then envision failure, and list behaviors that interrupted or deflected the course of success. After sufficient discussion, finalize a short list of behavior guidelines you think are critical to the mission. It is extremely important that every single member of senior leadership buys into these behavior guidelines. Ultimately, senior leaders will need to hold the entire organization accountable for living the guidelines—starting with themselves. Halfhearted attempts at defining behavior guidelines will go nowhere. As stated earlier, if you are not personally energized about behaving according to the guidelines, do not engage in the exercise.

I have seen too many companies with lofty value statements that mean nothing to people. This happens when senior leaders don't hold themselves, or anyone else, accountable. Steve Kerr, whom we met in chapter 4, often uses an interesting exercise in his training programs. Ahead of a program, he asks participants to send him their company's values or business principles. During the program, he puts all submissions in a show box and pulls a couple out at random. He then tells participants that he is going to read out a few, and requests them to raise their hand if the one he reads out belongs to their company. To everyone's surprise, each time he reads out one company's values, several hands are raised. They all sound so similar and lifeless that executives cannot even recognize them. Most companies establish values or principles. Very few manage to make them a way of life as American Express or Starbucks did.

SOCIALIZE

The next step is to socialize the behavior guidelines. Here, leaders lead by example, and at every step of the way must demonstrate the guidelines or values through their own behavior. Humans are hierarchical beings. Right from when we are born, we take our cues from those in a position of authority above us and behave accordingly. If mom and dad preach the importance of behaving in a certain way but do nothing to either encourage the behavior or punish the lack of it, we quickly learn that it is not so important after all. Leaders who lecture about the importance of teamwork and collaboration in normal times, but blame others when something goes wrong, send a very clear signal to their people—that the most important thing here is to watch your own back. So this second step of socializing—communicating and demonstrating the importance of the cultural values you want to establish— should not be underestimated. Leaders need to take every opportunity to communicate the guidelines and make people understand why they are important.

Effective socialization happens in three primary ways. The most powerful is through actions rather than words. Very early in my career when I was a frontline employee at American Express Bank, I was working late one evening after most people on my floor had gone home. A phone was ringing repeatedly a few desks away, but since it was after hours, I ignored it. A minute or so later, Jim Vaughn, the country CEO who also happened to be working late, was on his way out of the building when he heard the same phone ring again. I will never forget when he walked up to the phone and asked the caller what he could do to help. Without telling the caller that he was the CEO, Jim took down a detailed message and assured the caller that it would be communicated to the intended recipient as soon as possible. Before hanging up, he thanked the caller for calling American Express. You might think this is a trivial and obvious example, but for me, a twenty-two-year-old employee, it was a lifelong lesson about customer service. Leaders should use every opportunity to exhibit desired guidelines or values in their own behavior.

The second way to socialize the desired culture is through training. At American Express, every employee had to attend training to fully understand the essence of the American Express brand, and how to live the blue-box values every day. Senior leaders of the company routinely showed up at these training sessions to show employees how important the values and brand were. It was hard to be at American Express and not believe in them. At Coke, too, the brand is a religion, and employees regularly receive training on the value of the brand. In sharp contrast, I was with a client at another company recently and we agreed that his company should launch a mandatory session for all senior managers about the strategy of the company, and about behaviors needed from each of them to enable success. My client was convinced that a deeper understanding of strategy and what leaders needed to do was absolutely critical to success, particularly in a difficult economy. We agreed that about forty two-hour sessions were needed to cover all senior managers. I suggested that a member of the executive team be present to facilitate each such session. People needed to believe the company had a winning strategy, and having senior executives tell the story in their own words would not only be powerful, it was absolutely necessary at the time.

I was surprised when he told me to design the session in such a way that it did not rely too heavily on the executive team's presence. He expected his internal HR people to team up with external consultants to deliver these important sessions. Even though this would be a lucrative piece of business, I advised him not to undertake such a big project if he thought the senior team would be unwilling to invest their time. He argued that the senior team was already under a lot of pressure, and that this would be a huge time commitment for them. I could not believe my ears. After all, as leaders, what do you spend time on if not on aligning your organization's culture with your vision and strategy?

The third way to socialize is through ongoing communication. A basic rule of communication is that you can never do too much of it. A common mistake I have observed among leaders is that they communicate something once or twice and believe the message got through to people. I will never forget an argument I once had with a CEO who had asked me to help him with creating a stronger culture of high performance within the company. After doing some data-gathering interviews, I went up to him and said people in the company did not understand the business strategy and that it was important that they did. He was very frustrated on hearing what I had to say because he had recently spoken at length about the company's vision and strategy at a minimum of five forums. He could not understand why people still did not get it. But even the most gifted of communicators must realize that every recipient filters information through his or her own personal frames of reference. While the information is the same, the message absorbed is different depending on the lens (frame of reference) through which it is filtered.

The only way to ensure that a message has been absorbed consistently is to communicate it repeatedly using different methods (like speeches, presentations, e-mails, videos, intranet tutorials). Don't worry about sounding repetitive. Use every means possible, and do it as often as possible.

REINFORCE

The final step toward changing or creating a culture is to reinforce the desired behavior guidelines or values. In essence, what leaders do here is bring home the point that living the values is important. This is by far the hardest of the three steps, one in which most organizations fall short. Ultimately, if you want to make sure people indeed behave according to stated guidelines and live the values, you must answer the WIIFM (what's-in-it-for-me) question. The three most important levers at your disposal as leaders here are performance management, compensation, and promotion. Controlling these three levers can ensure values are not just bullet points on a poster or in training modules, but are important elements for personal success on the job. In the previous chapter, I listed American Express and Goldman as two examples of companies that have done a good job of linking values-based behavior to compensation and promotion. Leaders must discuss the best ways of doing this at their own organizations, and communicate clearly how employees will benefit (or not) by living the values.

To summarize, the proactive management of your organization's nerves is extremely important. As I've said before, your culture can be the one strength your competitors cannot easily copy. In describing her own transition to enterprise leadership, Jacqueline Novogratz of the Acumen Fund said, "When I moved from being a founder to being a CEO, I realized that my title should be the chief culture officer. Now, besides fund-raising and managing the board, I spend most of my time storytelling—to constantly remind people about our mission, vision, and values."

If leaders do a good job of proactively managing the nerves of their organization, employees must strongly agree with the following five statements:

1. We have a well-defined cultural philosophy (who we are and what we stand for), and it is well understood by everyone.

2. Our compensation and rewards practices encourage desired behaviors in line with the cultural philosophy.

3. Through their actions, our leaders set the right example for others.

4. We focus on both short-term success and long-term capability building.

5. Our culture is one of listening, learning, and constant renewal.

BRAINS, BONES, AND NERVES (B-B-N): THE ONLY FRAMEWORK REQUIRED TO ENERGIZE YOUR BUSINESS

Ultimately, the job of the leadership team is to set direction, design the organization, and create a culture of long-lasting excellence. From time to time, leaders must step back and assess how they are doing at these three primary tasks of enterprise leadership. An excellent way to do this is to ask their employees to complete the B-B-N survey shown on page 156, and to convene a meeting of the leadership team to discuss the results. Strong leaders keep the lines of dialogue open—just as they are consistently communicating with employees about a vision for the company, they are also constantly asking for feedback and are not afraid of uncovering areas that need improvement. If this survey highlights the need for action, invite your team to own the solutions—remember your team members are your co-leaders.

Please read each of the following statements and rate your level of agreement on a 1–5 scale where 1 = strongly disagree, 2 = disagree, 3 = neutral, 4 = agree, and 5 = strongly agree

	SETTING DIRECTION (BRAINS)	RAT-ING
1	We have a compelling vision for future success	
2	We have a clearly differentiated strategy to achieve our vision	
3	Vision and strategy are so clear that they guide resource allocation and decision making	
4	We have clearly recognizable core capabilities that give us our competitive edge	
5	Everyone in the organization can clearly and consistently articulate our value proposition to clients	
	DESIGNING THE ORGANIZATION TO EXECUTE STRATEGY (BONES)	
6	We have top quality talent with the right skills and experience in all key jobs	
7	Our supporting systems and structures (e.g., performance management, promotion processes) encourage desired performance	
8	Roles, responsibilities, and decision rights are defined as clearly as possible	
9	Our people and resources are deployed in a way that best supports the execution of our strategy	
10	Formal organization structure enables building and strengthening our core differentiating capabilities	
	CREATING A CULTURE OF LONG-LASTING EXCELLENCE (NERVES)	
11	We have a well-defined cultural philosophy (who we are and what we stand for), and it is well understood by everyone	
12	Our compensation and rewards practices encourage desired behaviors in line with the cultural philosophy	
13	Through their actions, our leaders set the right example for others	
14	We focus both on short-term success and long-term capability building	
15	Our culture is one of listening, learning, and constant renewal	
	OTHER	
16	What is working well that we should continue and/or do more of?	
17	What should we do differently to be even more successful?	

I particularly like this B-B-N survey over traditional instruments used in leadership development programs. Most of them try to measure your leadership style, your personality type, or the color of your brain. This survey instead provides direct feedback on your actions as a leader on the three most important levers of sustainable growth— the brains, bones, and nerves. Feedback gathered is generally tangible and actionable. The data can be plotted on a simple profile and used as a backdrop for brainstorming.

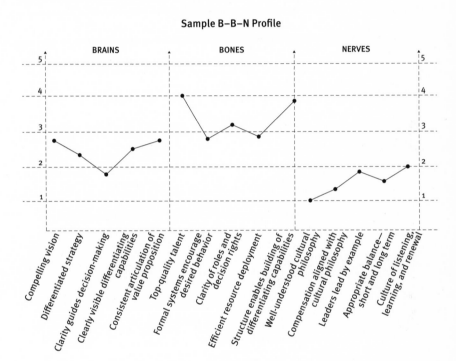

Sample B–B–N Profile

7

Common Threads,
Individual Paths

In chapters 1 through 6, I have tried to challenge conventional wisdom and lay out what I believe is the essence of effective leadership: harnessing human energy toward the creation of a better future. The journey begins with envisioning that better future, and requires incredible amounts of human energy to create it. Leaders must first uncover their own sources of leadership energy—their purpose and values—then enlist a few co-leaders and align their energy toward a common purpose. Finally, the leader and her co-leaders must galvanize the energy of the rest of the organization by shaping and managing the brains, bones, and nerves of the enterprise.

Throughout the preceding chapters, I have shared stories of great leaders to illustrate the methods that work through specific cases. In this chapter, I will share the stories of a handful of exceptional leaders to illustrate that while great leadership requires those three fundamentals listed above, every great leader must find his or her own particular mission and path to leadership, whether it be as an entrepreneur, a corporate manager, an educator, or a political leader. My hope is that these stories provoke ideas that you can use in finding your own path to great leadership. I begin with the fascinating story of Jeff Bezos, the CEO and founder of Amazon.com.

JEFF BEZOS

On November 17, 2007, when Amazon.com launched their first e-book reader—the Kindle—talk-show host Charlie Rose asked Jeff Bezos where the Kindle launch sat in relation to everything else Amazon had achieved thus far. Asked of someone like Bezos, it was a tough question. This man had already started the world's first online retail company, survived the dot-com crash, expanded from books to selling almost everything else on the Web, created a marketplace for third-party sellers, become a Fortune 500 company with one of the most recognizable brands of the Internet age, and started a company to explore space travel. Most of us would be glad to claim just one of those achievements in our entire lifetime. However, Jeff Bezos had no trouble responding without any hesitation, "What could be more meaningful than trying to improve the book? Books are the core of civilization." Watching that show, one could tell that Bezos meant what he said. Besides making the Kindle a commercial success, he had a bigger purpose as well—to transform the way people read, and to bring reading back into the lives of a lot of people who had stopped reading. Amazon's long-term vision for the Kindle is to make every book ever printed in any language available to readers in less than sixty seconds.

From a very young age, Bezos was clear about his passions. During his high school years, he wanted to become an astronaut. Space was an important part of his dreams, which were always big. He wrote a paper called "The Effect of Zero Gravity on the Aging Rate of the Common Housefly" as part of a NASA-sponsored student competition, and won a trip to the Marshall Space Flight Center in Alabama. He made no secret of the fact that he wanted to build a commercial space station someday. In his graduation valedictory speech and in a subsequent news publication, he described a vision that involved building space hotels, amusement parks, yachts, and colonies for millions of people orbiting the planet. No one would have believed at that time that this high school student with crazy dreams about space would one day actually start a company dedicated to developing vehicles and technologies that will, in time, help build an enduring human presence in space. Yet that is exactly what he did in 2000 when he founded Blue Origin. Some people believe he founded Amazon.com only to amass enough wealth to invest in his childhood dream.

After graduating with a degree in electrical engineering and computer science from Princeton, Jeff had no trouble finding work. By the time he was twenty-eight, he was making more than $1 million a year with D. E. Shaw, one of the most cutting-edge trading firms on Wall Street, and had twenty-four people working for him. At this time (the early nineties), hardly anyone had heard of the Internet even though the technology for interconnected computer systems had existed since the sixties. David E. Shaw was watching recent advances in Internet technology with keen interest, and asked Bezos to research Internet-related business opportunities.

Bezos soon learned that Web usage was growing at an astounding rate of 2300 percent a year. After looking at mail-order companies, he compiled a list of twenty possible items that could be sold on the Internet, including computer software, office software, and music. By means of careful analysis, he looked for answers to questions like what products would lots of people be willing to buy without actually seeing or handling them, and concluded that books would be best suited to start with. There were a number of factors that made sense: First, the book industry was highly fragmented—there was no dominant player in either book publishing or bookselling. Random House, the biggest U.S. publisher, had less than 10 percent of the market. Barnes & Noble and Borders had a combined share of less than 25 percent of the $30 billion book-sales market. Second, there were physical limits to how much inventory even the superstores could carry. The biggest Barnes & Noble and Borders stores carried an impressive 175,000 titles, but this number was still minuscule compared with the over 1.5 million English language books in active print. Online stores would have no limits to the number of titles they carried. They could easily acquire and ship any book from one of two main distributors. Third, most booksellers already had computerized inventories to keep stock, so a part of the work involved in setting up an Internet-based business was already done. Finally, the book business was inefficient. Publishers could never accurately predict how many books would sell, and often overprinted them. Returns (from booksellers to publishers) were a huge problem. Thirty-five percent of all shipments were returned in 1994. Not only this, but one of the most compelling arguments in favor of books was that everyone knew exactly what a book was, and retailers did not have to explain product features to customers. All of these factors made books an ideal candidate for selling "sight unseen" over the Internet. However, as convinced as he was about selling books on the Internet, Bezos could never convince his boss, David Shaw, about investing in the business. His strong conviction made him quit his $1-million-a-year job and move to Seattle to start Amazon.com.

Based on research, the decision to sell books to individual customers ("what" and "who") had been made. Now Bezos needed to answer the "how" and "why" questions. At this time, most pioneers of the soon-to-unfold new economy were grappling with the question, What is going to change because of the Internet, and therefore what should we base our strategy on? Bezos had a different idea. He asked, What will *not* change even in spite of the Internet, and what will be true even five, ten, or twenty years later? According to Bezos, there are three things that will never change about customer needs: low prices, vast selection, and accurate, fast, and convenient delivery.

In my opinion, this is where the genius of Jeff Bezos comes to the forefront. Someone with a strong scientific bent typically lives in the realm of science and technology, and typically approaches day-to-day problem solving through a scientific lens. Despite his impressive background, which includes a double major in electrical engineering and computer science, and a lifelong love affair with science and technology, Bezos approached the strategy ("how" and "why") questions from the lens of customer needs. He asked, What do customers (book lovers) want today, and will continue to want well into the foreseeable future? Again, after an analysis of customer needs, the answer was clear and ultimately became (and still remains to this day) the basis for Amazon.com's strategy. Bezos often says, "I cannot imagine customers saying five years from now that Amazon.com is great, but I wish their prices were higher. They will always want low prices, a very large inventory to choose from, and a convenient way to receive their books on time." I am not suggesting that technology was not important at Amazon; it was. The difference is, technology is an enabler, not an end it itself. A lot of technology-focused people tend to make the mistake of doing the reverse.

First, Bezos focused on the selection of books as the product to enter the online retailing market, then he focused on simple customer needs—the strategy could not be easier to understand. Everyone at Amazon knew exactly what to do when they understood the "what," "who," "how," and "why" questions. They were to build the biggest repository of books on the Internet, and to do everything in their power to give customers great service, quick delivery, and reasonable prices. It is no surprise that Jeff Bezos then went on to build what he calls "the most customer-centric company in the world." From hiring the right people (bones) to creating a strong culture (nerves) based on a few core beliefs, Bezos carefully built Amazon one day at a time. From day one, people who were invited to work at Amazon would generally need two qualities: They would have to be experts in their field of work, be it software design or inventory management, and also be high achievers in one other area, such as music, art, or sport. The idea behind this was simple: If someone has excelled at music or sport, it is proof that they have the tenacity to work long and hard in addition to having raw intelligence. Hiring was, and still is, something Bezos spends a large proportion of his time on.

The basic beliefs of the company have not changed since the early days, and are reflected in the company's values. Right from the early days, Bezos built the company's culture by modeling the behaviors himself and demanding the same from those who worked with him. Unlike other places, values were a way of life at Amazon. This is how they are posted on their Web site:

We make decisions as a company, and as individuals, based on our core values:

- **Customer Obsession:** We start with the customer and work backwards.

- **Innovation:** If you don't listen to your customers you will fail. But if you only listen to your customers you will also fail.

- **Bias for Action:** We live in a time of unheralded revolution and insurmountable opportunity—provided we make every minute count.

- **Ownership:** Ownership matters when you're building a great company. Owners think long-term, plead passionately for their projects and ideas, and are empowered to respectfully challenge decisions.

- **High Hiring Bar:** When making a hiring decision we ask ourselves: "Will I admire this person? Will I learn from this person? Is this person a superstar?"

- **Frugality:** We spend money on things that really matter and believe that frugality breeds resourcefulness, self-sufficiency, and invention.

Notice the words of the opening sentence: "We make decisions as a company, and as individuals . . ." The whole point of having values is that people make decisions based on them. Take innovation for example. In its short history, Amazon already has a number of firsts to its credit, largely because innovation was encouraged at every step of the way. People were expected to listen to customers and regularly find ways to innovate. The results of such a culture are clearly visible. Not only was Amazon the first online retailer, it was also the first company to introduce "one-click checkout." After establishing itself as the largest online retailer, Amazon opened up its platform to third-party sellers to set up storefronts on the Web site, thereby creating a whole new revenue stream. And more recently, with the launch of the Kindle, the company is reinventing the book-reading experience. As a friend of mine, a senior executive at a commercial bank, commented recently, "Thanks to the Kindle, I have started reading again." At the time of this writing, Kindle is less than two years old, and it already accounts for 35 percent of all book sales on Amazon.com. Besides making money for the company, the Kindle is creating a better future—one in which more people are reading, and fewer trees are converted to paper. Finally, with Blue Origin, his space company, Bezos continues to experiment with his childhood dream. Innovation and invention have always defined Jeff Bezos, and they have become a way of life at Amazon.

Whichever way you look at it, Amazon.com is a story about leadership. From personal energy based on purpose and values, to enlisting the energy of a few co-leaders that helped create the Amazon phenomenon, to galvanizing the entire workforce toward creating the Amazon experience for millions of customers every day, the real power behind this company is not science, technology, or capital, it is leadership. In a 2009 interview with Steven Levy, when he was asked about entrepreneurship and invention, here is what Jeff Bezos said:

> One of the differences between founder-entrepreneurs and financial managers is that founder-entrepreneurs are stubborn about the vision of the business, and keep working the details. The trick to being an entrepreneur is to know when to be stubborn and when to be flexible. The trick for me is to be stubborn about the big things.

There are a few prerequisites to inventing . . . You have to be willing to fail. You have to be willing to think long term. You have to be willing to be misunderstood for long periods of time. If you can't do those three things, you need to limit yourself to sustaining innovation . . . You typically don't get misunderstood for sustaining innovation.

If you substitute the words "founder-entrepreneurs" with "leaders" in the first quote, and the word "inventing" with "leading" in the second quote, you have the perfect list of requirements of leadership as described in this book.

TOM GARDNER, CEO OF THE MOTLEY FOOL

A couple of years ago I had a financial adviser from a major Wall Street firm manage my money. My relationship with him lasted about two years. I established an IRA (U.S. retirement) account and a retail brokerage account with the firm through this adviser. At the time of establishing my accounts, he asked me what my investment goals were. I told him in plain English that I did not care if I made much money or not, but I did not want to lose money on my retirement account. I said I didn't care if I missed all the exciting opportunities, but wanted the most low-risk investment strategies. As long as I could make marginally more than what the funds would earn in a savings account, I would be happy. I also told him that I would manage the brokerage account myself, and would place buy or sell orders with him whenever I wanted to trade.

I am no expert at investing, but generally like to keep a small amount of money aside to occasionally buy and hold stocks that I think might do well. Besides not having any particular expertise or insight into investing, I also don't have the time to monitor my investments on a regular basis. I tend to use common sense to buy or sell, and often mistime the market because I am not always on top of things when it comes to financial news. Yet, at the end of the first twelve months of working with my financial adviser, my retail brokerage account was up 30 percent and my retirement account was down 35 percent. When I questioned my esteemed adviser about the performance of my retirement account, he responded proudly by saying I was doing better than the market, which was down 40 percent. When I reminded him about my investment goals and demanded to know why I was paying him a management fee, he had no real answers for me. The final straw came when I sent him an e-mail asking his opinion about 2328.hk—a Hong Kong listing that I was interested in. I asked him to send me some research on 2328.hk. To my absolute horror, I received a quick reply asking, "What is the ticker symbol please?" Needless to say, I immediately closed both my accounts.

Unfortunately, my situation tends to be the rule rather than the exception when it comes to the retail money-management industry. Only about two or three out of ten retail financial advisers turn out to be any good. Most advisers are completely commission-oriented and are only interested in maximizing the number of trades. What makes matters worse is that the average person like me is either not knowledgeable about managing finances, or does not have the time to manage his own finances, or both. Schools and colleges around the world do an inadequate job of making people smart about managing money. It is a big gap in present-day education systems. To make matters worse, reading or watching financial news is both drab and tiring. The financial media seem to specialize in making things complex and boring. It is against this backdrop that in 1993, brothers Tom and David Gardner started a company they called The Motley Fool, taking the name from Shakespeare, whose wise fools both instructed and amused, and could speak the truth to the king without getting their heads lopped off. The whole purpose of the company is to educate the average investor and help him make better decisions about his money. They do this by providing newsletter subscriptions, investment advice, money-management services, creating online investment communities where people learn from one another, and through books and newspaper columns.

The company's Web site (www.fool.com) lays out their mission, vision, and values as follows:

Mission: To educate, amuse and enrich
Vision: To build the world's greatest investment community
Core values: Honesty, optimism, teamwork, innovation, winning

I had heard a lot about what a great place to work The Fool was. Everyone described it as a "fun" place. I had also been reading and enjoying their newsletters over several years, and always wondered why the Gardner brothers were so evangelical about educating retail investors. I could not understand why someone as skilled as they were about financial markets would spend their time educating rather than investing for themselves. To find out, I visited CEO Tom Gardner at the Virginia headquarters of The Motley Fool. From the moment I entered the office, it seemed like a company with a different attitude than most. The two receptionists were dressed in jeans and sweatshirts, and seemed to be thoroughly enjoying whatever they were doing behind their computer screens. When Tom's assistant came out to get me, she, too, was dressed in blue jeans and a T-shirt. I finally met Tom, and he, too, sported jeans. He also wore a baseball cap on his head with the letters *F-O-O-L* running across the front. They all seemed energized and happy—a rarity in most offices in the financial services industry.

To begin our conversation I asked Tom to tell me the purpose behind The Motley Fool, and how it had become his purpose. He explained that there were two main reasons for starting the company. One was the fact that he and his brother had learned about investing from their father when they were teenagers, and they wanted to pass on this gift to as many people as they could. The second was the brothers' love of people, communication, and entrepreneurship. "On a typical morning during our family spring vacation," he explained, "our father would, instead of playing tennis or swimming, take us to meet the CEO or

CFO of a company in the area to learn about their business. We were extremely fortunate to have learned from our father. Upon finishing college, we wanted to do something entrepreneurial, and we thought, why not educate people about investing, and we started our first newsletter." In response to my request to say it in a few sentences, he summarized the strategy and purpose of the company as: "People pay us to provide financial and investment advice that is predominantly distributed online, and includes a community debate about that advice. So we are in essence a membership business and we provide our services in a fun way."

I spent an entire afternoon at The Motley Fool to find out if this was really a *leader-led* (as opposed to *boss-led*) company. In the end, I walked away convinced that everything I had heard about The Motley Fool was indeed true, and that it was a company of leaders rather than bosses. To begin with, I wanted to know more about the mission— "to educate, amuse and enrich." I could understand "educate" and "enrich," but what was "amuse" all about? Educating the retail investor about managing his money well was novel enough a goal for the financial services industry, but these guys also wanted to amuse their audience? It did not seem to make sense until Tom explained very simply. "The problem with reading financial literature or watching financial news on television is that it is about as much fun as going to the dentist," he began. "Finance is a terrible subject. Conventional wisdom in the financial services industry suggests that the audience for investment advice is small, mostly made up of ultra-high-net-worth individuals. The industry takes itself too seriously. Most bankers dress beautifully in elegant suits and work in very slick offices. At The Fool, we dress casually and believe in having fun. Because of our love for people, we wanted to reach out to a much larger audience. We wanted as many people as possible to learn what our father had taught us, and realized that if we wanted to reach a large audience, we needed to make the subject fun and amusing. We thought about our teachers in school. Some classes were so drab that we somehow just wanted to get through and figure out how to write the paper. Others were fun and lively, and we waited to attend them. Those were the ones we learned the most from. We fashioned The Motley Fool after our favorite teachers."

Given how rare such ideas are in the financial services industry, I still could not understand why Tom and David wouldn't just invest for themselves and a few clients in order to maximize their own wealth. In all my years in the banking industry, I had not come across anyone who did not want to get rich as quickly as possible. Why spend time on a low-margin activity such as educating others? It didn't seem to make sense until Tom explained. "We started right after college and we were very oriented toward education. We went to great schools, and so it was a natural extension for us. As I said earlier, we also love people and communication, and the idea of sitting behind a computer in an office making money for ourselves and for our clients was not nearly as attractive to us as the ability to interact and learn from our clients in a scalable way," he said. He also explained that the goal for The Motley Fool was to remain successful for a hundred years. The Gardner brothers are more interested in building an organization that provides great investment advice year after year than in maximizing their returns in the short term. When I asked what they meant when they said they wanted to build "the greatest investment community," he said they wanted to ensure three things. One, to provide investment advice that is usable, and therefore changes behavior. Two, to make sure the advice is the most rewarding over the long term. Three, to do it in a fun and engaging way. I was struck by the crispness of Tom's responses. That he was very clear about his purpose, and the purpose of the company, was abundantly clear to me.

When I asked Tom what he looks for when selecting members of his direct reports' team, his answer was people who have curiosity and self-awareness, are self-starters, and have a sense of humor. "If they are curious, they will get smarter over time. If they are just brilliant, the brilliance could wane over time. We like people who will get smarter over time. For this, self-awareness is a must. People need to be aware of their strengths as well as weaknesses. Unless people can acknowledge their weaknesses, they cannot grow. Finally, I like self-starters largely because I am not much of a hands-on manager," he said. Just like Jeff Bezos, Tom was very clear about the type of co-leaders he wanted to invite on the journey. He knew clearly the kind of company and the kind of environment he wanted to create, and looked for co-leaders who would be willing to make the vision a shared one. While he wasn't exactly using the RED terminology, he was definitely using the ideas behind it. For instance, by looking for "people who will get smarter over time," he was looking into development, the *D* of RED.

Switching gears, I asked Tom what he thought were the keys to long-term organizational performance. Again, he replied without hesitation, telling me that there were three:

1. A mission and purpose that people can believe in (*the* brains, *in our parlance*).

2. In their individual roles, employees within the organization have challenges that excite them (*the* R *of RED*).

3. Employees have great people to work with (*the* E *of Red*).

"Even though they are the most important drivers of long-term growth, no company does a committee-level review of these three things. Every company has a board-level committee for compensation and bonuses. This has to do with the short-term nature of markets. Shareholders want a 50 percent return in two years, not a 13 percent annual return over twenty years. This intensity has influenced companies to focus on monetary issues rather than on issues that create long-term health and success. Instead of looking for short-term returns, we want leaders who want to grow The Motley Fool, and themselves, in a healthy way over the long term," he explained.

Whether I was asking about purpose and values, or about how he recruits and manages his direct reports' team, Tom always spoke about building long-term success. I could not help but notice the similarity to Jeff Bezos, Howard Schultz, Jacqueline Novogratz, and several others I had studied or met. They were all playing for the long haul. Even when I tried to find out how he makes sure his immediate team is motivated and energized all the time, he started by reminding me about his desire to make The Motley Fool successful for over a hundred years, and explained that pacing and flexibility is more important than "always-on" motivation and energy. "If we are really serious about the hundred-year idea, we have to understand that nobody can be fully engaged and energized at all times. Odd as this may sound, I orchestrate de-motivation," he said. "If someone has a family issue, I want them to disengage from the office and take care of the family issue. We want to provide the maximum flexibility and pacing possible so that over the long term, people are as motivated as possible. I don't want to make the maximum-possible money over the next three years and become unviable in ten years. I don't want my leaders to live a highly unbalanced life and get burned out in a few years.

"We don't have a vacation policy here," he continued. "People just take vacation when they need to and for as long as they want. But we have a review every ninety days." Imagine a company that does not count vacation or sick days. Clearly, not many had abused this privilege at The Motley Fool.

This reminded me of the way Steve Kerr—my boss at Goldman Sachs—would assign work within his team. He would bring up new projects at his regular team meetings and ask people to volunteer if they were interested. I once asked how the work would get done if no one volunteered. After all, everyone wants to own the sexy projects but no one likes the dull, routine ones. Steve promptly replied that in his thirty-plus years of managing people, he had never had that problem. He had experienced several instances of the reverse—i.e., some people took too much on—but never a situation when no one volunteered. "You can take the entire ninety days off if you like, but no one ever does," said Tom Gardner while explaining The Motley Fool's theoretically unlimited vacation policy. I asked how he finds out if someone has a family issue or if someone wants a change, and he said he never stops asking his people how they are doing. Again, I could clearly see

RED in action. As you will recall from chapter 2, one of the key ideas behind RED is to keep a constant dialogue going with your team.

Another tactic Tom uses to motivate his team is to provide them with change and with stretch assignments. It is common for people to switch responsibilities at The Motley Fool. Someone running HR today could run the membership business in a couple of years and vice versa. Besides providing change and stretch, which in turn motivate people to do their best, this switching also creates greater appreciation for others' work and reduces conflict.

To close our fascinating discussion, I asked a few questions about the future of The Motley Fool. First, I wanted to know why people would continue to choose The Motley Fool over other providers, and again he had no hesitation in responding. "Three reasons," he said. "One: We've built a reputation over seventeen years for being honest and transparent. We've earned their trust. Two: We've performed well as investors over the seventeen years. And three: We are becoming, and have the potential to be, the most convenient option for people. The Internet is only just beginning to show its real impact. It takes fifty years for a technology like this to show its real impact on society and on organizations. We believe much of the financial advice in the future will be given over the Internet via live streaming video."

Over the next few years, the company aspires to expand internationally and grow its new fund-management and financial planning businesses. Keeping with their mission, they are breaking new ground in the fund-management business by tying their fees to performance. "You want to pay us more if you are an investor with us," explained Tom. The idea is simple. If the fees the company earns are linked directly to the success of the investment ideas provided, the more successful clients' investments are, the more the company will earn in fees.

At 3 p.m. I noticed a lot of people walking out of the office. It was a bright sunny day outside. I asked Tom what was going on, and he explained that between 3 and 4 p.m. every day was recess time at The Motley Fool. "Don't you remember how much you loved recess time at school?" he asked. "Most offices have windows that never open. Every-one needs vitamin D, and the sun is the most common source of it. Our people sit indoors behind computers all day. They don't get enough sunlight. This is why we have recess time. We want our people to love coming to work, so we take great care in designing a culture in which people are excited." I asked how he would describe the culture, and he said, "Supportive, competitive, and energetic—the place is alive!" Could it be true? A financial services company that *is alive*? It certainly seemed to be the case at The Motley Fool. I wanted to know how senior management finds out if people are living the values or not, and Tom explained that there were predominantly two ways of doing it. One is the quarterly review process. Everyone gets a quarterly performance review. The other is the open-office architecture. Everyone sits at an open workstation, there are no offices, and it is therefore difficult to hide anything. That said, he did admit that they could get a lot better at specifically focusing on living the values.

I had seen all the evidence I needed to conclude that leadership is alive and kicking at The Motley Fool. Tom told me that they were well on their way to repaying the $50 million they had raised in the nineties to fund the business. It was heartening to see them succeed based on solid leadership principles.

ALAN MULALLY: FROM BOEING TO FORD

In November 2008, when the heads of the three big U.S. auto compa-nies appeared before the U.S. Senate committee considering a bail-out for the industry, the future of Ford looked bleak. Ford's stock was down to $1.43. For years, its offerings had failed to generate much excitement, with dealers and customers equally confused by the com-pany's lineup of eight brands: Ford, Mercury, Lincoln, Jaguar, Land

Rover, Aston Martin, Volvo, and Mazda. Thanks to a series of acquisitions over several preceding decades, by 2006 the company was producing over a hundred models. Further, production had become increasingly complex. For instance, a Ford Focus made in Europe was constructed in a markedly different way from one in the United States. Even a comparison of two U.S. models yielded few similarities—there was no definable "feel" to a Ford-produced automobile. Brand Ford had lost its meaning. For years, the finance department had primarily run the company. According to the *Detroit News,* the accounting section controlled the budget, and product developers picked up the habit of making unsupported sales and revenue projections in order to tell accounting what it wanted to hear in order to secure the budgets needed. In addition, features were actually removed from cars before they arrived in showrooms in order to meet budget constraints. Needless to add, employee morale was it its lowest, and the culture could best be described in one phrase: "cover your ass." There was hardly any sign of teamwork, innovation, or ownership.

Despite this gloomy picture, in November 2008, Ford was in much better shape compared with GM and Chrysler, largely because of one thing the company had done right in recent years—hiring Alan Mulally from Boeing as its president and CEO. Mulally acknowledged in an interview with the *Detroit Free Press* soon after his hire, "We are not competitive, and it has been getting worse year after year, forever." The first leader selected from outside the industry, Mulally came on board in late 2006 with years of questionable Ford management decisions to overcome. The most immediate problem: Customers were staying away in droves. But after Ford recorded a $2.7 billion gain in 2009, its first annual profit in four years, it would seem, so far, as though Mulally has performed miracles. He also brought Ford its first bump in U.S. market share since 1995, and according to a February 2010 *Wall Street Journal* article, internal surveys showed that more than 85 percent of Ford's workers thought the company was on the right track. At the time of this writing, the upward momentum seems to be continuing with healthy profits already in the books for the first two quarters of 2010.

Before being hired by Ford, Mulally was in the midst of a decades-long career at Boeing. He started at the company in the engineering department in the 1960s just out of college, and moved up through the ranks, gaining experience with all of its 700-series aircraft models (especially the 777) to become the company's EVP and the CEO of the commercial air unit. He is the man credited with bringing the company back from disaster after the 9/11 terror attacks forced a major contraction in the public's appetite for air travel, thereby resulting in major cutbacks by the airlines. By 2003, although aircraft deliveries had dropped dramatically from 560 as recently as 1998, to 280, the company had regained profitability. Close to 60 percent of Boeing's employees had been shed by mid-2004, in part a necessary correction to a workforce bloated during the late 1990s boom times. Incredibly, at the same time, Mulally sliced the average plane's build time in half. Unlike what is typical after a massive layoff, morale among the troops that remained did not suffer much, thanks primarily to Mulally's clear direction and transparency, and his habit of personally engaging with as many employees as possible at all levels. People understood that he had no choice, and further, they felt that the action pained him personally.

When Mulally appeared alongside Rick Wagoner and Bob Nardelli (then CEOs of GM and Chrysler, respectively) at the Senate hearing in 2008 to make a case for a government bailout of GM and Chrysler even while Ford did not need the money for itself, it was clear that he was a leader with a difference. On the face of things, it seemed absurd for him to help his competitors in their plea for bailout money. But Mulally looked at the systemic implications of the collapse of GM and Chrysler and knew it was time for the industry to stand together. For the industry to remain viable and healthy, it was important that GM and Chrysler survive. Several ancillary businesses such as original equipment manufacturers (OEMs) depended on all three of the big auto companies to derive their economies of scale. There are not many leaders in the world who have the foresight to think beyond their own companies about the broader ecosystem. Alan Mulally clearly did.

At the heart of Mulally's success throughout his career has been his very strong personal foundation for leadership. The foundation is made up of his ability first to energize himself with a deep sense of purpose and values, and with that, the magnetism to energize others. "I am here to save an American and global icon," he said when he first arrived at Ford, and he has not taken his eyes off that personal purpose ever since. According to a story carried by *Fortune,* many at Ford agree. His Americas team head, Mark Fields, has said, "Whenever I meet with Alan, I come away with more energy than I walked in with." Manufacturing head Joe Hinrichs concurs, "Alan brings infectious energy. This is a person people want to follow." Bill Ford, who selected Mulally, had this to say: "Alan is not a very complicated person. He is very driven." Indeed, Mulally describes himself simply: He "expects the very best of himself and others, seeks to understand rather than to be understood."

When he joined Ford in September 2006, one of the first things Mulally realized was that an impending downturn of the U.S. economy, and subsequently the global economy, would make it extremely difficult for Ford to survive without a stockpile of cash to tide it over the difficult times. Based on this foresight, he mortgaged off many of the company's assets in order to secure a $23.6 billion loan. While it was just smart business to prepare for a winter with very few nuts on the ground, this early action is what prevented Ford from asking for federal bailout money for itself in November 2008 when the great recession was already unfolding. When asked in an interview at the 2010 Consumer Electronics Show (CES) if Ford's resurgence and recent success had anything to do with not asking for federal funds, Mulally said he believes Ford's relatively strong position compared with its competitors gave people confidence in the company and its cars.

Once the financial resources needed to resuscitate Ford were secured, Mulally systematically began the rebuilding process. One of his early moves was the establishment of the "One Ford" concept. Through the decades, Ford was busy doing what any major industrial organization did—it grew both organically and through acquisitions, picking up fancy nameplates like Aston Martin and Jaguar. But in the process, it had lost the basic premise of Ford. Mulally's mission was to find this again. He saw an incredible opportunity to build up the brand by applying all of the energies and strategy that had been expended on the rest of the company's stable. By 2010, he had sold many of Ford's prestige holdings, like Jaguar, Land Rover, Volvo, and Aston Martin, and cut the number of models in production from over one hundred to twenty-five. He saw this focus as necessary in rebuilding the Ford brand. As a first step, the CEO decreed that the disparate processes and parts—turn signals, ignitions, door locks, and the like—in use throughout Ford's operation would be streamlined and standardized as much as possible. Thus, as of 2013, there will be fewer than ten international production platforms instead of the more than twenty regional ones that existed previously.

According to a May 12, 2009, *Fortune* story, in one early management meeting, Mulally was examining Ford's product roster and felt a bit stymied. He said,

> I arrive here, and the first day I say, "Let's go look at the product lineup." And they lay it out, and I said, "Where's the Taurus?" They said, "Well, we killed it." I said, "What do you mean, you killed it?" "Well, we made a couple that looked like a football. They didn't sell very well, so we stopped it." "You stopped the Taurus?" I said. "How many billions of dollars does it cost to build brand loyalty around a name?" "Well, we thought it was so damaged that we named it the Five Hundred." I said, "Well, you've got until tomorrow to find a vehicle to put the Taurus name on because that's why I'm here. Then you have two years to make the coolest vehicle that you can possibly make."

Fast-forward two years, and the totally remodeled 2010 Taurus was rushed to dealers in the summer of 2009 to healthy U.S. demand and high marks from industry watchers. Furthermore, the first new, wholly "One Ford" offering, the 2011 Fiesta B-class (bred of European stock), is all set to debut in North America at the time of this writing in 2010.

So what does "One Ford" mean? The company had already

embarked on its big turnaround plan (the "Way Forward"), which was heavy with plant closures and layoffs but did not offer much in the way of strategic refinement. Mulally developed the "One Ford" mission, composed of simple, direct, and easily understood "expected behaviors":

Foster functional and technical excellence
Own working together
Role model the values
Deliver results

Any corporation can—and many do—issue mission-statement cards to all its employees. But the sentiments have to mean something to the employees and constituents, or the card is just a piece of laminated paper in the back of a wallet. The difference here is that Mulally created his "One Ford" mantra after speaking with employees from all areas of the company in order to find out what they thought the Ford name meant, or should mean. As Mulally put it to just-auto .com in 2009: "Three years ago we pulled everyone together, inside the company and outside the company, the investors, the employees, dealers, suppliers—everybody, around this same plan that we took to the banks. And so all the stakeholders were included. I am so proud that three years later we have improved dramatically and our trajectory is very positive. You can't move up in their eyes unless you are starting to include them as a partner, starting to share with them the production data, you're including them up front in the design—all the things that are important to them to let them be successful. They're very pleased with us."

It is easy to notice that in actuality, Mulally was just following the "$Q \times A = E$" mantra of maximum effectiveness. His strategy was simple: Construct a definitive, thorough, quantifiable message (quality), deploy it with simplicity, and secure employee engagement (acceptance) by involving them at every stage. With the "brains" of Ford rewired, the "bones and nerves" needed to be fixed as well. Over time,

the size of the company had grown faster than the ability of its directors to guide it; similarly, the organization's patchwork structure,
which needed to be restitched with each new acquisition, had become
unmanageable. The result was a company in which every department
head acted mostly independently and where "cover your ass" was the
name of the game.

In one of the first meetings with his senior leaders, each report
recounted how well the leader's section was doing. After everyone was
finished, Mulally asked, "You guys, you know we lost a few billion
dollars last year [2005]. Is there anything that's not going well?" One
manager then spoke up, explaining that technical problems had fore-
stalled production on the Ford Edge—and after a beat, the new CEO
applauded and thanked him for his candor. With that, he began building a culture in which everyone had the license to discuss problems
without fear of retribution. The new culture brought the focus to where
it should be—finding and enabling solutions. He instituted a weekly
meeting (the Business Plan Review) similar to what he had done all
along at Boeing. Every functional head is invited to this meeting, with
Human Resources and IT leaders regarded as equals to those from
manufacturing and development. Departmental operations reports
are coded as red, yellow, or green to denote how well they're functioning. "Everyone has to know the plan, its status, and areas that need
special attention," Mulally told *Fortune*.

With his new weekly meeting schedule, Mulally began a much
more inclusive and collaborative culture that was focused on one
thing alone—improving performance. Along with the forced equality
came enforced respect: No one is permitted an aside conversation, a
peek at the BlackBerry, or any other distraction while the meeting is
running. Mulally will stop the briefing cold and, it's said, won't think
twice about removing someone who can't follow the rules. He also
won't tolerate staff that does not get along at the expense of the mission. Another unique aspect of the meetings is their transparency. The
executives are permitted to bring guests (e.g., plant workers), who are

introduced to the attendees at the start. At the conclusion of the meeting, Mulally personally greets guests and solicits their thoughts on how to make their area (or the company) a better place. He also took the time early on to eat among "the masses" in the regular cafeteria, and continues to answer all his own company e-mail.

Mulally sees the future Ford as something of a moving living room, an environment that will allow the consumer to be plugged into all his usual digital experiences while keeping the driver as undistracted as possible. According to Molly Wood, an executive editor at CNET.com, Mulally announced (at the 2010 Consumer Electronics Show) a slew of enhancements to the SYNC technology jointly developed with Microsoft a few years ago, like the API (application programming interface) that will lead to iPhone-like mobile apps that work with the in-car SYNC system. Apps like Pandora and Stitcher, both enabling free Internet radio, and OpenBeak, that lets you get your Twitter feed read to you, will be the first few applications that owners of Ford cars will be able to download. Mulally also described Ford's upcoming "cockpit," the MyFord Touch system, which is a highly connected car interface that will start appearing in 2011 models.

In just three years, Mulally has redrawn the brains, bones, and nerves of Ford from a sleeping giant to a nimble, high-tech company. It was the government's Cash for Clunkers program that brought buyers to Ford showrooms in the summer of 2009, but Mulally believes it is Ford's reputation that keeps them coming. For the month of February 2010, Ford shipments topped GM's for the first time since 1930 (except for two periods in 1998 and 1970 when GM workers were on strike). The automaker has clearly seen the error of its ways, and is now operating much more effectively. Both GM and Ford were insular, complicated organizations, their executives territorial and old-fashioned. Ford is in the process of shedding those constraints—there's a new focus on creating transparency within the organization, and a new mantra ("One Ford") that centers on quality of product and the wants of its customers.

MAURA COSTIN SCALISE—
HARVARD WOMEN'S SWIMMING COACH

For good reason, sports are a common metaphor in business, particularly golf, crew, and mountain climbing. But it would be hard to find a better and more timeless illustration of how great leadership inspires and empowers performance than Harvard Women's Swimming in 1983 when a twenty-six-year-old dynamo named Maura Costin Scalise arrived on the scene as the head coach.

The numbers tell part of the story. Before Costin Scalise, in the nine years that the Harvard Women's Swimming team had been in existence, it posted a .50 win-loss record, including three seasons when the team was under .25 in wins. The year before Maura joined as head coach, the team went 0–4 against a soft roster of competition. Yet Maura, in her first year as head coach, posted a winning season of 8–4. The next year, her team went 11–2 and was undefeated in the Ivies. In her third season, her team posted a perfect 11–0 record swimming against tougher competition and was good enough to compete in the NCAAs against the traditional swimming powerhouse colleges.

The statistics continue: By the time that Maura left after thirteen seasons, her teams posted an astounding 105–20 win-loss record (still the best ever in the Ivy League), won the Ivy League title seven times, had a four-year undefeated winning streak in the Ivies, won the larger and more competitive Eastern Championships for the first time ever— then repeated that win three more times—went two seasons undefeated, and achieved the best finish ever in the program's history (ranking seventeenth in the country at the NCAAs).

Maura's ability to embed success deeply into the enterprise was so complete that the team continued to win even after she left in 1996/1997 to enter business—she now runs a family-owned nursing home in her hometown of Nahant, Massachusetts. In the eleven seasons since Maura left, Harvard Women's Swimming has stayed on top and posted a combined record of 79–17.

The story behind Harvard's dramatic turnaround had nothing to do with a bigger budget, better equipment, or newer facilities. It came down to leadership and Maura's ability to instill a new, winning culture. And its takeaways are as universal and applicable to business as they were in a pool.

From a prominent Massachusetts family with strong Harvard ties, Maura herself graduated from Harvard in 1980. A competitive swimmer since the age of six, Maura was used to setting high goals for herself. Twice the Y national champion in the 100 free, she qualified for the Olympic Trials at age twelve and was the state champion in that event in high school. Maura knew from the time she was a teenager that she wanted to coach swimming and stayed focused on that goal. Heavily recruited by all the Ivy League schools and offered swimming scholarships at several traditional swimming powerhouses, Maura chose Harvard, where she was named Ivy Swimmer of the Year while a freshman and majored in psychology because she felt it would help her in coaching.

Determined to get the best preparation for her goal, after graduation Maura became the assistant coach to one of the top coaches in the world, Don Gambril. Gambril was then the head swimming coach at the University of Alabama and in 1984 became the head Olympic swimming coach. After she coached for Gambril for three years, the job of head coach of Women's Swimming at Princeton became available and Maura was offered a three-year contract. However, her dream had always been to return to Harvard as the head women's coach and she heard that the Harvard job might also be opening up shortly.

At twenty-five years of age, Maura walked into the office of the Harvard athletics director and announced, "If the job of head women's coach is opening up, I want it. My dream is to take Harvard Women's Swimming from the bottom and put it on the top." Flabbergasted, the athletics director listened as Maura continued, "You need me. I can transform this team. But I also have an offer to coach at Princeton. If

I take it, I will stay at Princeton and build a team that you will never beat."

While it is important to make sure that a boast is supported, articulating bold goals is a prerequisite for exceptional performance. By this point, Maura's self-confidence was well grounded. She had the strong technical skills from working under one of the best, knew personally what it was like to perform at the highest levels, and knew where to find and attract the top people (in her case, swimming recruits). Maura also knew the unique "corporate culture" of the Harvard organization and understood the special restrictions and challenges she would face there. Maura believed that she held all the pieces, had all the reasons to believe in herself, and, most importantly, believed she could inspire the people around her to believe in themselves as well.

The team that Maura inherited when she first started at Harvard in the fall of 1983 was smart in the library but not fast in the water. Maura knew that the swimmers didn't have Olympic potential, but she also knew they had potential to be much better. To her, that was key. It would take better training, which she could provide, and the right attitude. But first and last, the team had to believe in themselves. At her first team meeting in September, she started working on her team's self-confidence. She told her swimmers that she believed in them and knew that they could swim faster, work harder, and have more fun.

Turnarounds take time, and the bigger the turnaround, the greater the amount of time. In the case of a collegiate sport, the assumption is four years—the length of time it takes to recruit every class making up the team. In her first year, Maura had persuaded a couple of star swimmers to enroll at Harvard instead of a traditional swimming powerhouse. Meanwhile, the rest of the team was posting personal bests on a regular basis. The women had gone from dejected losers to athletes who relished the chance to rise to the occasion. While Harvard was swimming in a meet against Brown midway through the season, the Brown Women's Swimming coach pulled out all the stops. Brown was then the top Ivy swimming power and ranked number twenty in the country, particularly impressive for an Ivy League school, with higher academic standards and tighter training restrictions. In Maura's experience, it was common in the Ivy League that once a team was obviously winning, it took it easy on the losing team by entering swimmers in off-events or putting backup swimmers on the relays. But Brown's coach didn't do that. He continued to swim his star swimmers in their best events to win with the largest margin. After her team lost to Brown 51–90, Maura went up to him. "That wasn't nice of you to run up the score like that," she said. He was unsympathetic and made it clear that he wanted to beat a woman coach by as wide a margin as possible. Unwittingly, he had thrown down the gauntlet that provided even more incentive to Maura for the next year when they would meet.

That next year, the Harvard-Brown swim meet took place at Harvard, and Brown made a statement by leaving half its swim team at home, including their best swimmers. Maura had decided to use the meet to make a statement as well. She strategized the team's training so that they peaked for that meet against Brown. After they handily won 83–57, Maura said to Brown's coach, "I guess a woman can beat you after all."

The team's next meet was against Yale, another Ivy League powerhouse. By now, her team had earned the respect of their competitors. "Yale saw how we beat Brown and they peaked for us," Maura recalls. "But our team believed in themselves. And we beat Yale as well." Those two wins against Brown and Yale were the turning point. Now it wasn't just the team who believed in themselves, it was everyone they swam against as well. So what made it all possible? What did Maura do differently as a leader? It boiled down to three things.

The first and most important was to build an atmosphere of trust, friendship, and, above all, hope. Maura's arrival as coach itself was a source of hope for the team. When someone of Maura's caliber as a swimmer told the team how strongly convinced she was about their ability to turn around, they were energized. As with business managers, some coaches motivate by fear and by channeling aggression and anger. As in business, sometimes it works. Maura did the opposite— seeking to create a clanlike environment of trust, open communication, and mutual support. Joining Maura's team required buying into her coaching concept: that the team was a surrogate family, much in the way that employees at many top businesses have to buy into the company culture. To support this, Maura developed a set of rituals and traditions to build trust, empowerment, responsibility, and openness. As she explains, "When there was a problem, the women would sit on the truth chair to discuss it. We had a rule: Whatever was said on the truth chair stayed there. Afterward, it was forgotten and helped clear the air." Before meets, each swimmer stood up and announced her individual and team goal to everyone. She had to put herself on the line. It didn't have to be a time. It could be something like, "I'm going to do a great turn or a great start."

"Before a competition, we did skits about the other team. We designated a girl who was very busy outside the pool with academics, a social life, and enjoying Harvard to the fullest as the 'Cosmo Queen.' We had dinner-dance banquets at my house and everyone knew it as a great time. The boys were lining up to be invited. Before a championship meet, I'd have the girls come out to my house for a pajama breakfast, even driving out in their pajamas. I encouraged them to play pranks. One time, they didn't want swim practice and tied all the swimsuits together and draped them as a flag across the pool." Maura continues, "I wanted the girls to have fun and for them to look forward every day to going down to the pool. Swimming became more than swimming. I wanted to help develop these young women to be better people, believe in themselves, and know anything is possible."

The second thing Maura did was to make a change in training techniques. Because of Ivy League restrictions, her swimmers could train in the pool only two hours a day, while swimmers at the top national swimming schools trained five hours a day. Maura had to made adjustments for the Harvard culture, even though it put her at a disadvantage against the top competition. But like a business manager facing tight budgets or other resources, she concluded, "We had to use our hours wisely and get in as much as we could while working with what we had." She developed individualized training incorporating the latest techniques for starts, turns, and dry-land training with weights. Individualized training was then common in the top swimming powerhouses but not in the Ivy League. Before Maura, the entire team trained the same way. But Maura took the time to develop separate workouts for each swimmer, based on personality, inclination, abilities, specialty event, and personal swimming goals. While explaining the new training routines, she commented, "Now we might have swimmers with different workouts swimming in the same lane."

The third thing was the way in which she recruited swimmers. Maura's hiring philosophy was unusual and at the core of her philosophy on leadership: She didn't aim to recruit the best swimmers possible. Instead, she targeted swimmers who were good but hadn't trained under the most sophisticated programs, hadn't yet peaked, and so could be better. Her reasoning? She didn't want burned-out swimmers on the downslope of their careers, even if they were fast. She wanted swimmers who could transition to Harvard swimming, with fewer training hours than at their top competition. Most importantly, she wanted to instill a culture of progress and excitement—where every swimmer was training hard, willing to put herself on the line, improving, having fun, and being supportive of the other swimmers. Maura explains, "My goal was to pick the swimmers who were willing and capable of improving, and who would become winners when they got there. If someone has been swimming at the top levels for twelve years before Harvard, when she gets to Harvard, she often discovers that the school offers her so much else beyond swimming. She often loses that excitement for swimming." By picking swimmers who had not yet peaked in talent or in interest, Maura was able to foster an environment where her team was always looking forward to achieving a new personal best.

As the three changes began to take root and the team continued its success, Maura was able to recruit more women who were both tops academically and also top swimmers. In a domino effect, the team now got invited to compete in the most challenging invitational meets and push themselves further at the highest level of competition against college swimming powerhouses such as universities of Alabama, Georgia,

Texas, and UC Berkeley. Success in the pool also made fund-raising outside of it much easier. Unlike at major swimming colleges, fund-raising is a key part of an Ivy League coach's job. Having a winning team—let alone a dominant one—always makes raising money easier. Now Maura could afford better training trips to more exciting venues such as Hawaii, the Virgin Islands, and Barbados—in turn, also helping attract the more desirable swimmers. By the third year under Maura's leadership, Harvard Women's Swimming was a national power.

At a swimming meet at Yale one year, the score was so close that it came down to the last event, the 4 x 100-yard relay. If Maura's team won that relay, they would win the Ivy title outright for another year. But the leadoff swimmer was sick and could barely complete her four laps of the pool. By the time the anchor leg was ready to dive in, Maura's team was already behind by a full lap. It all came down to that anchor leg. Maura told the woman who swam the anchor leg what time she needed to post for the team to win. As Maura puts it, the time "was so fast." It represented a huge improvement over the woman's personal best. "A full lap is a ridiculous amount for a swimmer to make up," Maura comments. Yet she believed in her swimmer and said to her, "You can do it."

The swimmer replied back, "Yes, I can." And then she did.

As different as the fields of endeavor and the particular achievements of each of those leaders are, their stories have the fundamental of superior leadership in common. Each begins with a deep desire to make a difference—a strong sense of purpose and values. Once energized with his or her purpose and values, each enlisted a few co-leaders on the journey, and together they spent most of their time shaping the brains, bones, and nerves of their organizations. The result in each case was an organization whose collective energy was channeled into standout results.

8

Nurturing the Most Valuable Intangible Asset

In considering the seemingly unstoppable success of Apple Inc. in recent years, one wonders how much of it is directly attributable to the leadership of CEO Steve Jobs and what will happen when he steps down. Clearly, when he went away for a few months of medical leave, the market was jittery about Apple's stock. Similarly, how much of Google's success can be attributed to its top leaders? In earlier chapters, I talked about Harvey Golub at American Express and Howard Schultz at Starbucks. Along with head of HR Joe Keilty, Harvey rebuilt American Express into a solid corporation in the 1990s. Today, when we think about the Amex brand, words like "reliability," "exceptional service," and "prestige" come to mind. To what extent was Harvey and Joe's leadership responsible for what we know to be the strengths of American Express today? Like Steve Jobs, when Howard Schultz left Starbucks for a period of time, the company began to lose its way. After his return, it found its feet again. How should we value Schultz's leadership?

A perhaps related question we should ask is this: How much of a company's stock price is made up of intangibles such as the company's brand value, its ability to innovate, its culture and reputation, and the quality of management? Arguably, all these intangible assets are the direct results of the company's leaders' actions over the years. According to analysts, the answer is over 65 percent. In other words, when buying a stock, investors pay for expected future value, which is created by intangible assets—that part of a company's worth made up by its staff (its human capital) and their skills, knowledge, and creativity. According to an analysis by Professor Malcolm McDonald in his paper "Linking Invaluable Assets to Share Price," in 2006, when P&G paid £31 billion for Gillette, only £4 billion of that price was made up of tangible assets. The remaining £27 billion (87 percent) was paid for intangibles such as brand value and the company's ability to innovate.

The point I am trying to make is simple: If intangible (future) value is a direct result of leaders' actions, are corporate leaders of today doing enough to maximize it? With some exceptions, I don't believe they are.

Whether you are a senior manager or CEO, or at the beginning of your journey to leadership, it is important to understand the value of two vital and interrelated senior management responsibilities: leadership development and succession planning. The best leaders take both of these seriously, and with both there are best practices that will ensure the proper development of leadership talent and the future of strong leadership that will sustain, and continue to grow, a company's value. For excellence in both these areas, leaders must be prepared to challenge some conventional wisdom.

The first way in which this must be done is in the choice of the HR leader and the understanding of the HR function. The big problem is this: Even though it is widely acknowledged today that strategically managing human capital, designing and maintaining a strong organizational culture, and better understanding how to capture the imagination of the millennial workforce are critical to the success of any organization, key Human Resources positions are routinely filled without adequate thought. Even today, senior business leaders in many organizations use HR as a place to park loyal executives for whom there is no other place in the organization. They (the senior leaders) take the view that Human Resources is largely an administrative func-tion, and all you need to run it well are good administrative, legal, and accounting skills. The truth, however, is that a strategic HR partner can be instrumental in significantly enhancing growth because he or she directly influences 65 percent of the value equation—the intangibles.

This insight was not lost on Harvey Golub, Neville Isdell, and many others who have used Human Resources as a strategic plank. More leaders need to do so, and the first step is to choose the right HR leader, someone who can help as well as challenge them. Instead of choosing a comfortable confidant, they should look for someone who understands both business and human capital trends, and is able to contribute intelligently to C-suite discussions about business strategy. Far too many HR heads still do not have a seat at the table, and among those that do, very few have a voice. The only time they speak up is when there is a personnel-related crisis or an administrative issue.

Both the HR profession and the business leaders who appoint HR leaders are to blame here. I have already explained the tendency on the part of business leaders to choose someone comfortable, or to park someone they don't want to get rid of, in a senior HR posi-tion. HR executives, for their part, often don't do enough to earn their seat and voice. Many tend to thrive on reacting efficiently to requests from senior leaders, and are not proactive enough to support business growth. In this sense, many HR leaders are "pleasers." They feel hon-ored and important when a senior leader asks them to solve a ticklish issue involving a senior person's separation or a large layoff. They love it when senior leaders want them to draft policies for expense reduc-tion. By doing these tasks loyally and reliably, HR leaders earn the trust of their leaders. What they don't realize is that while they may have earned their leaders' trust, they do not earn their respect, which can only come from a proactive strategic contribution rather than from a reactive administrative contribution.

Ask most senior business leaders what they think about their com-pany's HR function and you will most likely hear something like this: "I hate HR, but I love my HR person. He is extremely reliable. Whenever I have a problem, I can trust him." Great, but is this all HR wants to aspire to? HR leaders should make a habit of staying on top of current and emerging business trends, and try to assess what might block the company's progress and determine the human capital needs of the company. Armed with knowledge in these two areas, they must proactively engage with senior business leaders by asking them critical questions and challenging them. Using the fifteen Brains-Bones-Nerves statements can be extremely helpful here. Each time I run a meeting for a senior management team to discuss data collected after conducting the ten-minute B-B-N survey, the feedback I receive tells me that I've surfaced issues that senior management should have been addressing all along but aren't. This is a simple but powerful example of how HR can add strategic value.

If HR leaders keep their eyes and ears wide open, they will discover things that are sometimes difficult for business leaders to perceive. For example, if a senior leadership team is divided on issues related to the overall strategy of their function, division, or company, the HR leader should be able to see it before anyone else, and should suggest to the head of the organization that he or she needs to do something about it. Better still, the HR leader should offer to run a strategic brainstorming session for the senior management team with a view to driving to agreement after all ideas have been heard.

Another case in which HR can add strategic value is that in which there is a disconnect between desired behaviors and the reward system. HR can study and suggest ways to bring better alignment between the two, thereby strengthening the organization's culture. Helping leaders manage large-scale change is another area in which HR can be instrumental. Finally, by providing practical and usable (instead of theoretical and mechanical) training and development programs, HR can help improve and accelerate performance.

All of this means HR needs to make some strategic choices for itself. Does it want to be the best administrative function in the world, or does it want to significantly contribute toward business growth? If the latter, it must decide which functions within HR are more important than others, and find the right balance between outsourcing and building in-house capability. An HR division that makes the decision to outsource all training and talent-management work while retaining full control of compensation and benefits sends a very different signal about itself than another HR division that outsources benefits and creates capacity for in-house consulting and leadership development. This might sound obvious, but I have heard far too many HR executives tell me that while training and other "soft" initiatives are nice to have, payroll, benefits, and other "hard" functions must go on regardless. Both HR leaders and business leaders must question themselves about the type of HR they want, and invest accordingly. In doing so, they should remember that in today's knowledge economy, technology, finance, or any other functional expertise can be copied or acquired. Excellence in the way a company manages its human capital can often make the difference between long-lasting success and failure. Companies like Goldman Sachs, Pepsico, Alibaba.com, Amazon .com, and Infosys, which are arguably some of the most commercially minded organizations in the world, agree. They all invest wisely in shaping their human capital strategies.

LEADERSHIP DEVELOPMENT

As I've argued throughout this book, leadership is not a matter of formulaic techniques, and it must not be cultivated by resorting to them. Leadership development programs should focus on helping participants understand who they are and what they want. As explained in chapter 1, for leaders to be authentic and effective, it is extremely important that they fully understand their emotions and their values.

George Kohlrieser, professor of leadership at IMD Switzerland and also my colleague at the ICLIF Leadership & Governance Center, concurs, and uses the most unique approach to leadership development

I have seen anywhere in the world. According to him, when development focuses too much on presenting the "how to's," the result is not deep enough to change the inner life of a leader. George makes the point that "most participants in leadership development programs already know more about leadership than they actually practice. Does it make sense to gather more knowledge and information without fully utilizing what you already know?" The heart of leadership development needs to focus, rather, on helping leaders find deeper levels of authentic energy to inspire their staff, build trust, create engagement, give hope, and help others reach deep within themselves to bring out their best. Intrinsic motivation is always more powerful than extrinsic motivation, and teaching leaders how to be extrinsic motivators, such as through the use of bonuses, has very limited value for sustained high performance.

George, who was a hostage negotiator for the New York police force for several years, places emphasis on developing emotional intelligence, which in my opinion is the missing link in today's leadership development activities. Here's how he describes the need for empathy in leadership:

> The world is changing faster than most of us realize. For leaders to be effective, this requires understanding loss, pain, frustration, fear, and uncertainty that so many employees have or are going through as a result of the rapid pace of change. This means recognizing when people are suffering and grieving over something they have lost or are anticipating losing, either at work or in personal life.
>
> The reality is that people experience the emotional process of grief every day on teams and in organizations over small as well as large matters. Sometimes small losses are more debilitating than large ones. In fact, the managers and the organization itself may be the source of that pain, loss, and grief. High-performing leaders are able to appropriately experience, and show, compassion to those who are in some stage of grieving. *Leaders must dare to care.* Traditionally, doing so was considered a weakness. Now, in the new world of leadership, it is a strength. Leadership training that guides leaders at all levels in understanding their own grief

in the form of professional and personal crucibles is at the cutting edge of high-performance leadership development. The fact is that those leaders who cannot form meaningful emotional bonds generally have some form of unresolved grief as part of the problem.

I cannot agree more. For leadership development to be useful, it must help people to pinpoint their own unresolved grief as a first step in showing them how to bond with others on a much deeper level.

SUCCESSION PLANNING

According to Tom Gardner, founder of The Motley Fool, one of the top reasons why companies do not achieve their full potential is that they do a poor job of succession planning, and bring their next leaders from outside. Outsiders, he believes, do not understand the culture of the organization, and hence it is no surprise that the company does not achieve its potential. In my opinion, it is not that companies don't have their next leaders within them; what it is, is that senior management does not create the conditions required for those leaders to show their leadership potential.

In many companies, succession planning ends up as a spreadsheet exercise to satisfy a board requirement. HR lists two or three possible successors for every key position, and senior management holds a meeting once a year to discuss what needs to be done to develop the potential successors. Typically, nothing happens beyond that. Some companies do better, and create development plans for each possible successor. Such plans typically include a mix of training, coaching and mentoring, and assignment rotation. Among the companies that are considered particularly good at succession planning are those that identify high potentials early in their career and give them developmental experiences to systematically prepare them for future leadership positions. Such identification and subsequent development of high potentials has been considered a best practice for some time now. I would like to offer a different perspective.

The question is, in today's rapidly changing world, does it still make sense to identify a few, anoint them as high potentials, and invest disproportionately in their development? What if the world changes in ways that require a totally different type of potential in five years compared with the benchmarks used to identify today's high potentials? What about late bloomers—those who may not show early brilliance, but might become very valuable later on? And what about the negative impact on the morale of those not chosen as high potentials?

For all of these reasons, it might be time to rethink the "best practice" of identifying and developing a pool of high potentials. Given the uncertainties of business today and the powerful forces shaping our lives—such forces as mobile and robotic technology, the globalization of the workforce, and changing demographics (for example, the aging populations in some parts of the world vs. a young and vibrant population in places like India)—it is impossible to tell who will be the thought leaders of tomorrow. Instead of putting all their eggs in one basket of early-anointed high potentials, companies should expand their chances of producing future leaders by giving everyone a similar development diet and letting the cream rise to the top on its own. Instead of treating a chosen few differently, companies can create meaningful development programs and options for all employees that allow them to show their strengths. For example, a good way to develop someone is to ask them to work on something in addition to their day job. Senior management can identify a list of strategic issues or opportunities it wishes to tackle, and invite employees to voluntarily create teams to address those issues. Only those employees who wish to participate will create a team. All senior management needs to do is set a few guidelines for participation, and leave the teams alone. If it wants to do more, it can provide a senior sponsor to each team who is willing to invest some time guiding the team, and perhaps even an executive coach, though this program works well even without the latter.

After the teams are allowed to work on developing their ideas for a few months, they should be invited to present their ideas to senior management. By listening to these presentations, senior management will automatically get a sense of who the best thinkers and performers are. By working on these teams, participants will get an opportunity to learn something that would not have been possible within the bounds of their day job, as well as to network with and get noticed by senior management. Doing programs like this annually can give senior management a very good view of their high potentials without anointing a few as such. It also reduces the risk of making mistakes while choosing the few. Because participation is totally voluntary and open, it does not create any morale issues for those left out. Another variation of this program is to leave the choice of topics to be studied up to the teams themselves. Anyone who has an idea that can save money, increase revenue, or improve any aspect of the company can be invited to form a team and participate in the program. Teams again develop their ideas and present them to senior management. The whole process is totally voluntary.

Another good way to select future leaders is to have a robust 360 feedback system in place. As mentioned earlier, Goldman Sachs as a firm spends a huge amount of time and money each year on their 360 feedback system. Each year, every employee receives 360-degree feedback. Over the years, the trends are clear—either someone shows leadership capability or they don't. Either they are a team player or they are not. When consistent over a number of years, the data does not lie. What better confirmation of someone's potential does a company need when ten years of 360 data clearly points to an individual's strength in leading others or at innovating?

At the end of the day, leadership is intrinsic. If someone takes proactive initiative to go above and beyond to create a better future, they are already showing their leadership ability.

AT A GLANCE: SUMMARY OF THE TOOL KIT

Why are there so few good leaders among us despite the huge invest-ment in leadership development?

Are leaders born or made? Is it possible to become a good leader if you are not one to begin with?

So what does it all boil down to?

THE LEADERSHIP VOID

Most people accept leadership positions without fully understand-ing what's involved, and without asking themselves if leadership is for them. Many underestimate the task of leading. The result is abun-dantly visible in every organization around the world: There are far too many bosses, but very few good leaders around.

We deem someone a leader when she achieves a feat that is diffi-cult for the average person. Leadership is the art of harnessing human energy toward the creation of a better future. Leaders must overcome significant obstacles, and succeed in spite of their environment, not because of it. By definition, therefore, leadership is hard. Furthermore, there is no guaranteed reward at the end. True leaders undertake the journey for the journey itself—the reward at the end is just the icing on the cake. Navigating all the obstacles and finding a way to succeed needs huge amounts of energy. You first need to find your own per-sonal sources of energy, and figure out a way to renew it regularly so

that you have staying power even in the face of the toughest of obstacles. You then need to mobilize the energy of others. It is all about energy, and energy can neither be learned in a classroom nor acquired through a big title or position. It must be discovered.

ENERGIZE YOURSELF

The leadership journey begins at home. The first step is to make sure you even want to be a leader, and why. You can do this by defining your purpose and your values. Defining purpose and values is essential for everyone regardless of whether they want to be a leader or not. For those aspiring to embark on the work of leadership, it is a must. Leadership is the work of creating results. Personal purpose enables one to toil toward a destination with conviction. The hard work and conviction sets a powerful example for others, and motivates them to participate. Without clear purpose, there can be no leadership.

If purpose defines the destination, values determine the route. Values form the personal belief system that guides behavior. If your purpose is to create wealth, there are many ways of doing it—some ethical, others not. If your purpose is to promote a cause, again there are many powerful ways of doing it—some peaceful, others violent. Clarity about your values helps determine which way you chose. Values are just as important as, if not more important than, the purpose itself. Not only are leaders clear about the results they want to create, they also know how they want to do so and at what cost.

The only way to energize yourself, and to sustain that energy in the face of unimaginable obstacles and difficulties, is to be clear about your purpose and values. Imagine that you have succeeded in creating the results you wanted to achieve. Does that visualization energize you? We have a lot of nonleaders in leadership positions because they have not clarified their own purpose and values. They live their lives reacting to stimuli rather than proactively creating a better future. If you are serious about energizing yourself for the long haul to be a leader, you need to be able to clearly answer the following six questions:

1. What three to five things are most important to me?

2. Do I want to:

    a. Lead a simple life rich with everyday small pleasures?

    b. Achieve great success in an individual endeavor?

    c. Lead others toward a better future? Or,

    d. Do something entirely different with my life?

3. What results do I want to create?

4. How do I want people to experience me?

5. What values will guide my behavior?

6. What situations cause me to feel strong emotions?

ENLIST CO-LEADERS (THE CORE TEAM)

Once you have built the foundation of leadership—your purpose and values—you can begin the journey of energizing other individuals around you one person at a time. Most managers ask themselves what they can do differently to motivate and energize their teammates. The first step in trying to do so is to turn that question upside down. Ask not what you can do, but what they want. Once you know the answer, what you need to do will automatically be clear.

While each individual is motivated differently, most have expectations from their workplace that fall neatly under three buckets. Everyone who works in a large organization has three fundamental questions:

1. What is my **Role**?

2. What is my work **Environment** like?

3. What are the prospects for growth and **Development**?

Energizing another individual is all about knowing her preferences under the three buckets of role, environment, and development (RED), and matching the work with those preferences. In general, people want the following statements to be true about R-E-D.

ROLE

- Our organization has a compelling vision for its future success.

- We have an effective/differentiated strategy to achieve the vision.

- I have challenging (stretch) but achievable goals.

- I clearly understand how my work fits into the overall vision and strategy.

- I have sufficient freedom and authority to do my job well.

- My role aligns with my personal purpose and values.

ENVIRONMENT

- My manager regularly engages with me and has a good sense of what is important to me.

- My opinion on important issues is sought and valued.

- Our organization has a culture in which people collaborate rather than compete with one another.

- Everyone in our organization is treated with respect and dignity.

- Our organization has an environment of community and friendship.

- Our organization has a fair reward and recognition system in place.

- Our organization has a culture of high performance where mediocrity is not accepted.

DEVELOPMENT

- I am given challenging assignments that provide me with opportunities to learn and develop.

- I receive regular coaching and feedback on my performance.

- My manager helps me identify my strengths and develop them further.

- Our culture strongly emphasizes entrepreneurship and innovation.

- Our organization constantly strives to upgrade its overall capability to deliver outstanding results.

- I am expected to come up with new ideas to improve efficiency and/or profitability.

GALVANIZE THE ENTERPRISE

Moving from midmanagement to an enterprise-level position is the hardest career transition. Three out of four careers derail or stall at this point. Only one in four people makes this transition successfully. For our purposes here, enterprise leadership means leading more people than you can maintain a direct boss–subordinate relationship with. In other words, you are an enterprise leader when you have a large organization with more than two levels of hierarchy reporting to you. A transition to an enterprise leadership position involves two changes. The first is learning how to stop "doing" and start "facilitating." Most people get promoted to a senior position because of their technical skills and/or direct revenue generation. Until this time in their careers, their own hard work produces direct results, and they get rewarded for those results. After they've spent a lifetime "doing," it is very hard to accept the fact that their job at the senior level is not about "doing" anymore. It is less about creating the results yourself, and more about creating conditions in which many others can create successful results.

The second change is a shift in your personal orientation. I call this shift from "I" to "We." At a senior level you need to get comfortable with the idea that you may not receive direct credit for results. Your job is to make others successful—that is hard work in itself, but you might not get credit for it at all. Again, clarity about your purpose and values helps in deciding if you want to (and can) make these changes successfully.

Once you've decided that you indeed want to make this transition, the next question is, What activities should you spend your own time on and what should you delegate? If a leader's job is to create conditions for everyone in the organization to be successful, how should he spend his time? If you don't think carefully about this question, before you know it, you will find yourself in the weeds of "doing" and will not be able to provide much-needed leadership to grow the business. My experience and research over the years has shown that the following three leadership activities provide the most leverage to an organization:

1. Setting direction *(the BRAINS of your business)*

2. Designing the organization *(the BONES of your business)*

3. Creating a culture of excellence *(the NERVES of your business)*

Proactively managing these three levers of a business is a full-time job, and enterprise leaders should delegate almost everything else. If a leadership team does a good job of managing these levers, employees in the organization should strongly agree with the following fifteen statements:

SETTING DIRECTION (BRAINS)

1. We have a compelling vision for future success.

2. We have a clearly differentiated strategy to achieve our vision.

3. Vision and strategy are so clear that they guide resource allocation and decision making.

4. We have clearly recognizable core capabilities that give us our competitive edge.

5. Everyone in the organization can clearly and consistently articulate our value proposition to clients.

DESIGNING THE ORGANIZATION (BONES)

6. We have top-quality talent with the right skills and experience in all key jobs.

7. Our supporting systems and structures (e.g., performance management, promotion processes) encourage desired performance.

8. Roles, responsibilities, and decision rights are defined as clearly as possible.

9. Our people and resources are deployed in a way that best supports the execution of our strategy.

10. Formal organization structure enables building and strengthening our core differentiating capabilities.

CREATING A CULTURE OF EXCELLENCE (NERVES)

11. We have a well-defined cultural philosophy (who we are and what we stand for), and it is well understood by everyone.

12. Our compensation and rewards practices encourage desired behaviors in line with the cultural philosophy.

13. Through their actions, our leaders proactively create a culture of collaboration and teamwork.

14. We focus both on short-term success and long-term capability building.

15. Our culture is one of listening, learning, and constant renewal.

Again, these fifteen items can be used as a quick survey to get feedback on leadership effectiveness. Data collected should provide good clues on what the team needs to focus more or less on, or do differently.

At the end of the day, leadership is about channeling energy. The best leaders energize themselves by defining their purpose and values, energize individuals around them one at a time by understanding and meeting their expectations (RED), and energize the enterprise by focusing on the three most important levers of a business—the brains, bones, and nerves. The following self-checklist is a good way to start assessing and defining your own leadership.

Please read each of the following statements and rate your level of agreement on a 1–5 scale where 1 = strongly disagree, 2 = disagree, 3 = neutral, 4 = agree, and 5 = strongly agree

I have clearly defined my purpose—what I want out of life	
I have a set of clearly defined values to guide my behavior	
I fully understand my direct reports' expectations and preferences regarding their Role, Environment, and Development	
My organization has a differentiated strategy to achieve our stated vision	
The strategy is widely understood by everyone in my organization	
My organization is designed to support the execution of strategy most effectively and efficiently	
We have the right people in all key jobs	
The culture of my organization promotes long lasting excellence	
My own behavior is in accordance with the culture we aspire to build within my organization	

Let me close by posing one final question: Are leaders born or made? I've thought long and hard about this question for many years, and here's where I have landed. Like any other task, good leadership is a function of *skill* and *will*. Can the skills of leadership be acquired if someone wants to learn them? The answer clearly is a big yes. Can the will be acquired? Some people argue that you either have it or you don't. However, looking at Mahatma Gandhi, Nelson Mandela, and Martin Luther King, we know that they acquired the will to lead when faced with a situation that they badly wanted to change. So yes, the will can be acquired, too, and you don't have to be born with it. I have concluded, therefore, that while some may be born, leaders can certainly be made as well.

Thinking about and defining your purpose and values should give you the *will* for leadership. Working first with individuals one at a time, then with the enterprise as a whole, as I have tried to describe in this book, should give you some ideas about the *skill*. At the end of the day, no one can teach you leadership—by using these ideas and tools, *you* will have to define what leadership means for you. If you go on this journey with full self-awareness, the rewards are endless. Good luck!

REFERENCES

INTRODUCTION

1. *Gandhi,* the 1982 biographical film produced and directed by Richard Attenborough and distributed by Columbia Pictures.

CHAPTER 1

1. Jacqueline Novogratz, *The Blue Sweater: Bridging the Gap Between Rich and Poor in an Interconnected World,* Rodale, 2009.

2. My personal interview with Jacqueline Novogratz at the New York offices of the Acumen Fund, December 2009.

3. www.acumenfund.org.

4. www.drishtee.com.

5. *Bodybuilding Universe: Arnold Schwarzenegger,* http://www.bodybuilding universe.com/arnold.htm.

6. Robert E. Quinn, *Deep Change: Discovering the Leader Within,* John Wiley & Sons, 1996.

7. Travis Bradberry and Jean Greaves, *Emotional Intelligence 2.0,* TalentSmart, 2009.

8. Daniel Goleman, *Emotional Intelligence: Why It Can Matter More Than IQ,* Bantam Books, 1995.

9. *Gandhi,* the 1982 biographical film.

10. Howard Schultz and Dori Jones Yang, *Pour Your Heart Into It: How Starbucks Built a Company One Cup at a Time,* Hyperion, 1997.

11. Howard Behar and Janet Goldstein, *It's Not About the Coffee: Leadership Principles from a Life at Starbucks,* Portfolio/Penguin Group, 2007.

12. A conversation with Starbucks Chairman Howard Schultz, *The Charlie Rose Show,* January 16, 2007, www.charlierose.com/view/interview/46.

13. A conversation with CEO of Starbucks Howard Schultz, *The Charlie Rose Show*, September 8, 1997, www.charlierose.com/view/interview/5372.

CHAPTER 2

1. My personal interview with John Mack, November 2009.

2. "Inside the Bunker: CEO John Mack on Saving Morgan Stanley," *Knowledge@Wharton*, October 14, 2009, http://knowledge.wharton.upenn.edu/ article.cfm?articleid=2357.

3. Andrew Ross Sorkin, *Too Big to Fail*, Viking/Penguin Group, 2009.

4. A conversation with John Mack, Chairman and CEO of Morgan Stanley, *The Charlie Rose Show*, February 23, 2009, www.charlierose.com/view/ interview/10095.

5. *Frederick Herzberg: The Two-Factor Theory and Project Management*, a knol by Steven Chong, http://knol.google.com/k/frederick-herzberg#.

6. http://en.wikipedia.org/wiki/Frederick_Herzberg.

7. Marcus Buckingham and Curt Coffman, *First, Break All the Rules: What the World's Greatest Managers Do Differently*, Simon & Schuster, 1999.

8. Liu Shiying and Martha Avery, *Alibaba: The Inside Story Behind Jack Ma and the Creation of the World's Biggest Online Marketplace*, HarperCollins, 2009.

CHAPTER 3

1. Jay Conger and David Nadler, "When CEOs Step Up to Fail," *MIT Sloan Management Review*, April 15, 2004.

2. Jim Collins, *Good to Great: Why Some Companies Make the Leap . . . and Others Don't*, HarperCollins, 2001.

3. Shiying and Avery, *Alibaba*.

4. http://www.alibaba.com/.

5. Jack Ma, *Economic Downturn Is "Growing Pain" of Globalization*, address to the Asia Society, March 2009, http://asiasociety.org/videos/ business-economics/jack-ma-complete.

CHAPTER 4

1. Elizabeth Corcoran, "Andy Grove's Re-entrance," *Forbes*, December 18, 2006.

2. Tina Wang, "Jack Ma's Five-Year Plan," *Forbes*, May 7, 2009.

3. My personal interview with Jacqueline Novogratz at the New York offices of the Acumen Fund, December 2009.

4. A conversation with Starbucks Chairman Howard Schultz, *The Charlie Rose Show*, January 16, 2007, www.charlierose.com/view/interview/46.

CHAPTER 5

1. My personal interviews with Kiran Bedi in 2008 and 2009.

2. Kiran Bedi, *It's Always Possible,* Indra Publishing, December 1999.

3. Kiran Bedi, *I Dare!,* Hay House India, 1995, 2009.

CHAPTER 6

1. http://finance.yahoo.com/.

2. http://www2.goldmansachs.com/our-firm/our-people/business-principles.html.

3. Coca-Cola Company Form 10K for fiscal year ended Dec. 31, 2007.

4. David McBride, "Lean Culture: The Toyota Culture of Continuous Improvement," *Learning to Lean,* http://www.emsstrategies.com/newsletter-070104article2.html.

5. Antoine Henry de Frahan, *How Toyota Is Rejuvenating the Idea of Corporate Culture*, 7/23/2007, http://www.frahanblonde.com/files/Toyota_corporate_culture.pdf.

6. Steven Rattner, "The Auto Bailout: How We Did It," *Fortune,* November 9, 2009.

7. My personal interview with Jacqueline Novogratz at the New York offices of the Acumen Fund, December 2009.

8. Coca-Cola marketing test settlement with Burger King, *Food & Drink Weekly,* August 18, 2003, http://www.allbusiness.com/retail-trade/food-beverage-stores/625596-1.html.

9. "SEC investigating Coca-Cola," http://bizjournals.com/atlanta/stories /2004/01/12/daily32.html.

10. "Coca-Cola settles SEC investigation, Isdell sends memo," http:// bizjournals.com/atlanta/stories/2005/04/18/daily7.html.

11. "Coca-Cola Settles Race Bias Case for 195.5 Million Dollars," http:// english.peopledaily.com.cn/english/200011/17/eng20001117_55480.html.

12. Bill Vlasic, "After Bankruptcy, G.M. Struggles to Shed a Legendary Bureaucracy," *New York Times,* November 12, 2009.

CHAPTER 7

1. Tim O'Reilly, "Jeff Bezos at Wired Disruptive by Design conference [Steven Levy interview with Bezos]," *O'Reilly Radar,* June 15, 2009, http://radar .oreilly.com/2009/06/jeff-bezos-at-wired-disruptive.html.

2. Ann Byers, *Jeff Bezos: The Founder of Amazon.com,* Rosen Publishing Group, 2007.

3. James Marcus, *Amazonia: Five Years at the Epicenter of the Dot.Com Juggernaut,* The New Press, 2004.

4. Bernard Ryan, Jr., *Jeff Bezos: Business Executive and Founder of Amazon .com,* Ferguson Career Biographies/Facts on File, 2005.

5. Robert Spector, *Amazon.com: Get Big Fast,* HarperBusiness, 2000.

6. Adam L. Peneberg, "The Evolution of Amazon," *Fast Company,* July/ August 2009.

7. A conversation with Amazon.com CEO Jeff Bezos, *The Charlie Rose Show,* November 17, 2007, http://www.charlierose.com/view/ interview/8784.

8. http://www.amazon.com/Values-Careers-Homepage.

9. My personal interview with Tom Gardner, CEO of The Motley Fool, February 2009.

10. www.fool.com/press/about.htm#mission.

11. Molly Wood, A conversation with Ford CEO Alan Mulally, January 8, 2010, http://news.cnet.com/8301-20966_3-10430683-262.html.

12. Alex Taylor, III, "Fixing Up Ford," *Fortune,* May 11, 2009.

13. Sam Abuelsamid, "Ford CEO Mulally Expects Many Fords to Be Electric in a Decade," AutoblogGreen, March 5, 2009, http://green.autoblog.com.

14. Sebastian Blanco, "Ford CEO Mulally Says Eco Factors Will 'Set the Agenda for Us All,'" AutoblogGreen, March 31, 2010, http://green.autoblog.com.

15. David Bowermaster, "Better Times, Fewer Jobs Ahead, Boeing's Mulally Tells Wall Street," *Seattle Times,* May 20, 2004.

16. Jim Buckman, "Ford Finds Its Way," *Quality Progress,* June 2009.

17. Nick Bunkley, "Ford Profit Comes as Toyota Hits a Bump," *New York Times,* January 29, 2010.

18. Jere Downs, "Ford Back in Black," *Courier-Journal* (Louisville, Kentucky), January 29, 2010.

19. Jere Downs, "Restructuring Helps Ford Post Profit Surprise," *Courier-Journal* (Louisville, Kentucky), July 24, 2009.

20. Addy Dugdale, *CEO Alan Mulally: Ford Still in Black but Also Green, Partners with Microsoft Hohm* [video], March 31, 2010, http://www.fastcompany.com//1602829.

21. Steve Everly, "Ford's Top Executive Tries to Rally Troops, Automaker's Future," *Kansas City Star,* January 27, 2007.

22. Dawn Gilbertson, "Unit Chief Optimistic about Boeing's Future," *Arizona Republic,* January 30, 2005.

23. Jane Hodges, "Boeing Shake-up Worries Local Employees," *Seattle Times,* December 3, 2003.

24. Bryce G. Hoffman, "Mulally Already Shaking Up Ford," *Detroit News,* September 22, 2006.

25. Paul Ingrassia, "Opinion: The Weekend Interview—Ford's Renaissance Man," *Wall Street Journal,* February 27, 2010.

26. Kevin M. Kelly, "A Leader When Detroit Needs One," *Automotive Design and Production,* May 1, 2009.

27. Bill Koenig, and John Lippert, "Cutting to the Bone: Ford Eliminates 10,000 More Salaried Jobs, Shuts Two Plants, Offers Buyouts to 75,000," *Chicago Sun-Times,* September 16, 2006.

28. Monica Langley, " 'The Plan' Is Mulally's Road Map to a Healthy Ford," *Seattle Times,* December 27, 2006.

29. Dave Leggett, "The Editor's Q&A: Ford's Alan Mulally," just-auto, October 30, 2009, http://www.just-auto.com.

30. Doron Levin, Ford CEO Alan Mulally interview on Bloomberg TV, *Analyst Wire,* January 18, 2010.

31. Joe Nocera, "Ford's Cheerleader and Chief," *New York Times,* May 23, 2009.

32. Alex Nunez, "Survey: Ford's Image Gets a Boost by Nixing Federal Aid," Autoblog, May 1, 2009, http://www.autoblog.com.

33. John O'Dell, "Ford Looks Down a Long Road Back," *Los Angeles Times,* September 17, 2006.

34. Maria Panaritis, "Ford Motor Co. Is Bouncing Back," *Philadelphia Inquirer,* February 7, 2010.

35. Steve Pearlstein, On Leadership Interview at 2010 Washington Auto Show, *Washington Post,* February 24, 2010.

36. Mark Phelan, "Job 1: Build Another Hit Like the Mustang," *Detroit Free Press,* September 17, 2006.

37. Jonathon Ramsey, "Mulally on Ford: 'We are competitive now?" Autoblog, March 30, 2009, http://www.autoblog.com.

38. Mark Ritson, *On Branding: Ford's Clarity of Focus,* May 27, 2009, http://www.marketingritson.com/documents/1fordsfocus.pdf.

39. Mike Rogoway, "Ford's 2009 Turnaround Profit," *The Oregonian,* January 29, 2010.

40. Alex Taylor III, "Fixing Up Ford," *Fortune,* May 21, 2009.

41. Bill Vlasic, "Ford Beats Estimates, but Claims No victory," *New York Times,* July 24, 2009.

42. Sarah A. Webster, "Sky's the Limit, Says Down-to-Earth Chief," *Detroit Free Press,* April 1, 2007.

43. Sarah A. Webster, "Upbeat but Realistic, Mulally Says Automaker Can Succeed, but Must Face Facts," *Detroit Free Press,* November 11, 2006.

44. Sarah A. Webster, "Ford to Critics: Our Plan Will Work; Jobs, Plants, Demand Set to Align," *Detroit Free Press,* September 17, 2006.

45. Brian White, "Ford to Gain More U.S. Market Share as Toyota's Mishaps Continue," BloggingStocks, March 15, 2010, http://www.bloggingstocks.com.

46. "Ford Topping GM Might be 'new normal.'" *Tampa Tribune* (Bloomberg News), March 4, 2010.

47. "New Ford CEO Used to Wielding Job Ax," *Grand Rapids Press,* September 19, 2006.

48. www.ford.com.

49. Susan E. B. Schwartz (research team member), personal interview with Maura Costin Scalise.

50. www.gocrimson.com/sports/wswimdive/history/year_by_year_results.

51. Susan E. B. Schwartz, telephone interview with Jeff Selesnick, Assistant Director of Athletics Communications, Harvard University.

CHAPTER 8

1. My personal interview and e-mail exchange with George Kohlrieser, December 2010.

INDEX

ABOUT THE AUTHOR

Rajeev Peshawaria is the Chief Executive Officer of the ICLIF Leadership & Governance Centre (www.iclif.org), based in Kuala Lumpur, Malaysia. A nonprofit organization focused on providing practical and usable leadership and corporate governance training, executive coaching, and leadership advisory services to corporations, nonprofit organizations, and government agencies in Asia, the Middle East, and Africa, ICLIF was recognized as Asia's best institute for leadership development in 2010. Prior to joining ICLIF, Rajeev spent over twenty years at blue-chip corporations in the United States, Europe, and Asia. He has served as the global chief learning officer at Morgan Stanley in New York, and at the Coca-Cola Company in Atlanta. At both companies, he created their respective corporate universities. He was one of the founding members of Pine Street, the renowned Goldman Sachs leadership development program, and was the global head of the firm's Leadership Advisory Services practice. Prior to Goldman Sachs, he was the global director of leadership development programs at American Express based in New York. Before embarking on a career in leadership development, he was a currency trader at American Express and HSBC.